LONDON'S HISTORIC RAILWAY STATIONS

Sir John Betjeman

Additional text for colour
section by Alan A. Jackson

Black and white photography
John Gay

Colour photography
Colin Garratt
James Whiting

Capital Transport

First published 1972
Second and enlarged edition 2002

ISBN 185414 254 2

Published by Capital Transport Publishing, 38 Long Elmes, Harrow Weald, Middlesex

Printed by CS Graphics, Singapore

Colour photography
Colin Garratt: photographs 3, 4, 5, 7, 8, 9, 14, 15, 16, 17, 19, 20, 24, 25, 26, 27, 31, 33, 35, 37, 38, 39, 40, 41, 42, 43, 50, 55, 56, 58, 59
James Whiting: photographs 1, 2, 6, 10, 11, 12, 18, 21, 22, 23, 28, 29, 30, 32, 34, 36, 44, 45, 46, 47, 48, 49, 51, 52, 53, 54, 57, 60, 61, 62, 63, 64, 65, 66

CONTENTS

PREFACE TO THE FIRST EDITION

LOOKING at railway stations can be as diverting as looking at old churches. The termini of a capital city are part of the lives of the nation, they witness the smiles of welcome, the sadness of goodbye, and many hours of compulsory boredom for the uninitiated. It was with the object of lightening the lives of those who have to use the London termini that this book was composed.

If the station houses – that is to say the waiting rooms and booking offices along the line – are the equivalent of parish churches, then the termini are the cathedrals of the Railway Age. Most companies, even if their origins were in provincial towns, were determined to make a big splash when they reached the capital. Only the luckless Great Central, that most comfortable of lines for passengers, ran out of money when it reached Marylebone, and was never able to complete a terminus worthy of the expectations raised by its buildings at Sheffield, Nottingham and Leicester. The individuality of the great companies was expressed in styles of architecture, typography and liveries of engines and carriages, even down to the knives and forks and crockery used in refreshment rooms and dining cars. Victoria is an architectural battleground of the rival railways to the South Coast, but the styles were always Classical until Modernistic came along after grouping in 1923. The Midland favoured Gothic, and so, in a less expensive way, did the Great Eastern. The great Western remained its strong Gooch-and-Brunel self. Greek learning dominated the London and North Western. The Great Northern went in for a reliable homeliness rather than beauty. Each of these railways had devoted and loyal staffs proud of the line, jealous of its rights and conscious of its dignity.

I am particularly obliged to Mr Bernard Walsh, Chairman of Wheeler's Restaurants Ltd, and publishers of *Wheeler's Quarterly Review*. The editor of this Review, Mr Antony Wysard, the artist, whose caricatures in colour and wash are such a feature of the late twenties and thirties, first proposed to me the idea of writing a series of illustrated termini. He too introduced the photographer, John Gay, who has the art of capturing the atmosphere and character of a place or building and of photographing significant detail.

As often happens when one is writing on a subject, another is writing on the same subject. When I was half-way through the railway stations, an excellent book, *London's Termini* by Alan A. Jackson, was published by David and Charles. As a factual and interesting history it could not be bettered and its author kindly agreed to read my text and make suggestions. Already, I suspect, both our books are mainly of historic interest, for the architects of British Rail never cease to destroy their heritage of stone, brick, cast iron and wood, and replace it with windy wastes of concrete.

As John Gay's photographs increased, I became aware that the rich inheritance of railway architecture from Victorian pride in achievement to Edwardian flamboyance, declining to the poverty of the new Euston, has a moral. There was nothing modern to photograph. There was much of the past which turned some of these termini into Cathedrals of industrial architecture. Moreover railways were invented and developed, to begin with, in Great Britain.

I hope that the photographs in this book will show the Minister for the Environment, who now has transport under his wing, that British Railways deserve a subsidy towards the maintenance of the splendid train sheds, offices, viaducts and tunnel entrances and station buildings, it has inherited. If landowners, clergymen and country house owners are entitled to endowment on architectural grounds, so too are British Railways.

JOHN BETJEMAN

PREFACE TO THE SECOND EDITION

JOHN BETJEMAN loved London and its railways, especially its railway buildings, with all their faults and eccentricities. Over 30 years ago he wrote *London's Historic Railway Stations*, a delightful book, sympathetically illustrated with some splendid and often witty black and white photographs by John Gay. Handsomely produced by John Murray, it was published in 1972. When copies surfaced on the second-hand market in recent years it is indicative of the high regard in which the author and his illustrator are held that the asking price consistently reflected a real increase above inflation.

This new edition includes an account of the major changes made in the last thirty years at each of the twelve termini which survive with important elements of their original structure. Not long after Sir John Betjeman's book was published, the climate changed to one more sensitive to the importance of conserving the Victorian and Edwardian architectural inheritance, obliging the landlords of railway property to pay regard to this concern as they sought to maximise their financial returns from commercial development of the station sites and air space. Sir John Betjeman died in 1984, too early to have seen any of these major development projects completed. It is interesting to speculate what he would have made of the interface between the two interests and its architectural outcome. There would surely have been at least one poem with plenty of wry comment and mischievous quips about the resurrection of Liverpool Street or the burial of Victoria.

ALAN A. JACKSON
Dorking,
April 2002

ST PANCRAS was a fourteen-year-old Christian boy who was martyred in Rome in A.D. 304 by the Emperor Diocletian. In England he is better known as a railway station. That station takes its name from the parish in which it stands. It is the terminus of the Midland Railway, the most mid-Victorian of all British lines. It wasn't the fastest line but it was the most comfortable, and was the first to introduce a dining car and upholstered seats for 3rd-class passengers. Its livery was scarlet. Scarlet were the famous Kirtley engines with their black funnels; scarlet the carriages and scarlet enlivened with stone dressings and polished granite the walls of the mighty terminus and hotel of St Pancras. So strong is the personality of this station to a Londoner that he does not remember the mediaeval but mercilessly-restored local church, nor the chaste Greek revival St Pancras church in the Euston Road, nor even St Pancras Town Hall opposite the station, now renamed Camden Town Hall. What he sees in his mind's eye is that cluster of towers and pinnacles seen from Pentonville Hill and outlined against a foggy sunset and the great arc of Barlow's train shed gaping to devour incoming engines, and the sudden burst of the exuberant Gothic of the hotel seen from gloomy Judd Street.

The Midland Railway did not reach London until 1867 for goods and 1868 for passengers. Its headquarters and its heart were always in Derby. It used to run trains into Kings Cross by arrangement with the Great Northern Railway. Its other rival from the Midlands was the long established London and North Western at Euston next door. This was always a belligerent and unco-operative company. If the Midland was to have a terminus in London, it must be a contrast with its neighbours – not old fashioned Greek and Graeco-Roman like Euston with its Doric portico and Great Hall, not mere engineering like grimy stock brick Kings Cross, but something to show that the Midlands and the Midland had plenty of brass and were not old fashioned. Bringing the line to London avoiding its competitors was difficult enough, and when the outskirts of the metropolis were reached it was harder still. After burrowing through the Middlesex hills at

Hampstead it had to cross a canal. Should it tunnel under this, as the Great Northern and the London & North Western had done, or should it cross it by a bridge? It decided to bridge the canal. In order to do this the very large and very crowded burial ground of old St Pancras would have to be levelled. When the work started, skulls and bones were seen lying about; a passer-by saw an open coffin staved in through which peeped a bright tress of hair. Great scandal was caused and the company was forced to arrange for reverent reburial. The architect in charge of the reburial was A. W. Blomfield, and he sent one of his assistants to watch the carrying away of the dead to see that it was reverently done. That assistant was Thomas Hardy, and his poems 'the levelled Churchyard' and 'In the Cemetery' recall the fact. Once when he and Blomfield met on the site they found a coffin which contained two skulls.

O Passenger, pray list and catch
Our sighs and piteous groans,
Half-stifled in this jumbled patch
Of wrenched memorial stones!

We late-lamented, resting here,
Are mixed to human jam,
And each to each exclaims in fear,'
I know not which I am!'

Hardy never forgot the event.

The Midland also had to clear a horrible slum district at Agar Town and part of the equally depressed Somers Town. The inhabitants were not properly rehoused. Yet on came the Midland, full of brass and assurance. It tunnelled one line down to join the Metropolitan (steam) Underground Railway, which is now part of the Inner Circle, and from Farringdon Street trains could enter the City or cross the river at Blackfriars. Most of its line at St Pancras stopped short at the Euston Road, but as it had had to cross the canal by a bridge, the station ended high in air above the Euston Road. This gave its engineer William Henry Barlow (1812–1902) a chance to build, what remained for nearly a century, the largest station roof in the world without internal supports. It also inspired him to build what is still the most practical terminus in London. The great cast-iron arched ribs

which support the roof were made by the Butterley Iron Company, whose name appears in white on a blue background on each rib above the platforms, reminding us of the Derbyshire origin of the line. The ribs are tied together by floor girders over which the trains run. To increase wind resistance the great curved arch of the station is slightly broken at its apex, so that it is almost a Gothic arch. This whole structure rests on a forest of iron columns under the station. The exterior fence of this forest is the brick wall of the station and hotel. The Midland made good use of the ground-floor level under its terminus. Much of the trade of the line was beer from Burton-on-Trent, and the distance between the iron columns was measured by the length of beer barrels, which were carried down here from the station above by hydraulic lifts, and taken by drays out into London. This gloomy area, when it ceased to be used for beer, became a lair of wild cats. It is now partly a National Car Park and partly the haunt of motor repairing firms. A few shops survive with Gothic windows to them along Euston Road and Pancras Road.

When Barlow designed the train shed, he made provision for an hotel to be built in front of it, above the Euston Road. The station and hotel are approached by ramps, one steep and the other a gentle double curve, so that to this day St Pancras is the most practically designed station for ambulances and certainly the most considerate and humane to mobile passengers.

The station was completed in 1868 and Barlow constructed glass screens at either end of his train shed. That on the Euston Road side was designed to keep smoke and noise from the projected hotel. The hotel was started in the year the station was completed, and it was opened to the public in 1873. At the time it was easily the most magnificent of all London hotels. It was one of the first to have lifts, called 'ascending rooms' and worked by hydraulic power. It was also one of the first to have electric bells. It could be a fine hotel again. The architect was the most eminent man of his time, Sir Gilbert Scott (1811–1878).

Sir Gilbert Scott was of course the envy of his profession. This is one of the reasons why the avant garde architectural critics of the 1870s condemned the building as a 'monster'.

Below Church Gothic
adapted to railway use
showing ornamental detail.

Right Gilbert Scott
delighted in making
ironwork part of the
architecture. Two views of
the ironwork forming part
of the Grand Staircase of
the Hotel.

It may also be a reason for the totally false rumour, which I once believed myself, that St Pancras was the Gothic design Scott made for the Foreign Office in 1856, and which Palmerston rejected. Having studied both designs and the plans for them, there is no resemblance except in style. It must be remembered that in the 1860s Gothic was the equivalent of what used to be called 'contemporary' in the 1950s. Any promising architect and go-ahead company would insist on Gothic if they wanted to be thought up to date.

Opposite Worthy of King
Arthur's knights. The foyer
of the Hotel.

For the last ninety years almost, Sir Gilbert Scott has had a bad Press. He is condemned as facile, smart, aggressive, complacent and commercial. When at the top of his form, Scott was as good as the best of his Gothic contemporaries. He was so firm a believer in the Gothic style as the only true 'Christian' style – Scott was a moderate High Churchman – that he was determined to adapt it for domestic and commercial purposes. St Pancras Station hotel was his greatest chance in London and well he rose to the occasion.

Right Symbolic capital. Trousers have been ever the bane of sculptors.

Below Roof of the train shed.

Opposite Sparrowhawk's view of the grand curve and sweep of the south facade. Note the importance of the skyline compared with the lack of it in the square slabs beyond, though, in the haze, the Post Office Tower struggles to compete.

I used to think that Scott was a rather dull architect, but the more I have looked at his work the more I have seen his merits. He had a thorough knowledge of construction, particularly in stone and brick. For St Pancras the bricks were specially made by Edward Gripper in Nottingham. The decorative iron work for lamp standards and staircases and grilles was by Skidmore of Coventry, who designed the iron screens in some English cathedrals for Scott. The roofs of the hotel are of graded Leicestershire slates; the stone comes mostly from Ketton. Scott's buildings are so well-built they are difficult to pull down. He had a grand sense of plan and site. The hotel building

Right Detail of the curve of the South Front, showing again Gilbert Scott's delight in ironwork.

Below Tiers of Gothic in Midland Road.

consists of refreshment and dining rooms at station level on the ground floor, and wine cellars in the basement. The Grand Staircase, which alone survives of the hotel's chief interior features, ascends the whole height of the building, by an unbelievably rich cast iron series of treads with stone vaulting and painted walls. The chief suites of rooms are on the first floor and the higher the building, the less important the rooms, until the quarters for the servants are reached in the gabled attics – men on one side, women on the other – and separate staircases. Yet even these are large and wide and compare favourably with more modern accommodation. The building has been chopped up and partitioned inside for offices. It is odd that it is not used again as an hotel especially now that hotels are so badly needed in London.

Scott had full confidence in being able to exploit the site. The chief rooms are on the front and look across to the once level plains of Bloomsbury and up and down the Euston Road. Even on the first floor they are sufficiently high to be out of the noise of traffic. For the external effect of his hotel Scott used the same technique as Barry had done for the Houses of Parliament, that is to say he increased the sense of height on the comparatively low setting by having a steep roof and many towers and spirelets. Such things always look well in our grey climate. He meant to put Euston and Kings Cross to shame. For the rear of his hotel, where it faced the station, he put service rooms and backstairs and made the brick exterior plain, since it was mostly submerged in the train shed. Above the train shed it rises into gables.

There was at one time a serious threat to St Pancras, both as a station and an hotel. Puritans of the 1930s were prepared to allow merit to Barlow's train shed, because it was simple and functional. Scott's hotel, however, filled them with horror, because its exterior was ornate and its style considered sham mediaeval. If you look again at the hotel you will see it is not sham. It uses brick of the best quality and cast iron, and its proportions bear no resemblance to a mediaeval domestic building – no mediaeval building, not even an Hôtel de Ville, of that size was ever built. There still

survive along the Euston Road some ingenious façades Scott has constructed for shop fronts in the low brick arches under the station.

Today we can appreciate Sir Gilbert's masterpiece. For grandeur of scale it compares with that best work of Sir Gilbert's grandson Sir Giles, Liverpool Cathedral.

The architectural department of British Railways has not tried to have St Pancras station cleaned, and has allowed mean hoardings for advertisements to deface the interior of the station, and to be placed without any regard for the vertical lines created by Scott and Barlow. Mingy little notices and cumbersome new electric lamps are stuck about without regard to proportion or the façades.

The now old-fashioned with-itry of the 1950s, which has given us the slabs and cubes of high finance, and ruined most of London, has made St Pancras all the more important to us for the relief it brings. It shows that trouble was taken and money spent in its building.

There is one more most important thing to be said in favour of St Pancras Station. This was said to me at a party I attended for the publication of Jack Simmon's readable, learned and inspiring book *St Pancras Station*. I was introduced to three former Station Masters of St Pancras, a succession going back to the 1914 war. They all said how magnificent the station was, how fond they were of it, and the last one added, "moreover *it works*".

Exterior of the great train shed, looking north, Britannia standing guard against lightning attack.

FOUR RAILWAYS in England had the prefix 'Great'. The biggest was the Bristol-inspired Great Western, which retained its character and name throughout the first days of the grouping of railways, and whose spirit nationalisation has not yet killed; the Great Eastern with its smoky suburban service and overcrowded second-class carriages; the Great Central glittering with 1890 luxury, the last main line to come to London; and the Great Northern, dogged and unassuming, by many the best-loved line of all. Those apple-green engines lined with black, crawled up the steep slope from Kings Cross through tunnels to Finsbury Park, carrying Londoners to Peterborough, Grimsby, York and Edinburgh. Britain's most famous train, the Flying Scotsman, made her last journey from here to the north, and was the subject of one of the best documentary programmes on television. From the days of Stirling's engines to those of Gresley's A1 Pacifies on the L.N.E.R. and the Great Northern Atlantics, Kings Cross has been noted more for its trains than its buildings. Of all London's termini Kings Cross is the least pretentious. It is an engineering job.

The engineers had a hard task to bring the line to the metropolis. Between Peterborough and Huntingdon it had to cross fen, and here it is said the track was built upon bundles of reeds and rushes. Certainly to this day the train makes a different noise between Fletton and Holme. In Hertfordshire it had to cross a valley by a magnificent brick viaduct at Welwyn; at Potters Bar it had to burrow through the Middlesex Hills. When it reached London, which it did in 1850, there was the Regent's canal to overcome before descending to Kings Cross itself from Holloway. They decided to burrow under the canal, and very narrow and steep are the three tunnels which were eventually made, down to the station. Today the blue fumes of diesel trail out of them, and when the wind is in the north they are blown, as the smoke used to be, through the waiting double mouth of the terminus, and come to rest at the inconvenient space where ticket collectors hold one up at the barriers.

Britannia surveys from Scott's St Pancras her simpler, earlier competitor Kings Cross.

Kings Cross Station was opened in 1852 and was built on the site of the London Smallpox Hospital. The engineer of the line was Joseph Cubitt (1811–1872) who built other London railways. His father, Sir William, was the engineer who invented the treadmill, and advised on the construction of the line. These Cubitts were relations of England's biggest and most successful speculative builders at the beginning of the last century. They flourished at a time when professionalism was only starting. The firm of Holland, Hannen & Cubitt is their survivor. Thomas Cubitt laid out Belgravia and built much of Eaton Square and of the Kemp Town end of Brighton, where his crescent and terraces are much admired. His brother William became Lord Mayor of London. There was one brother the others did not think quite so promising as the rest, and he was Lewis; so they decided to let him qualify as an architect with the new-fangled Institute of British Architects. He designed Kings Cross with the aid of Joseph Cubitt twelve years his junior. Like Telford and the Brunels, father and son, civil engineers were conscious of architecture as an art. They produced buildings of classical proportions, and were well versed in Greek and Italian styles. The Great Northern wanted its station put up quickly after the two-year delay, so there was no time for fal-lals.

Left Platform 8 departure side.

Below The train sheds seen from York Road (Up suburban) platform.

An early attempt at the functional.

The station could hardly be simpler in design. Two great round-arched train-sheds, one for arrivals one for departures: across them, on the Kings Cross Road, a severe brick screen, with a colonnade underneath it for carriages, and a clock tower in the middle, vaguely Italianate. On the departure side was a gaunt booking hall and a gloomy waiting room, which still exists. Alongside the station is the pleasant curve of the Great Northern Hotel, a Lewis Cubitt design, where he was obviously allowed to introduce a little more 'style', and here it is reminiscent of later Cubitt speculative building in Pimlico. The offices attached to the departure side of the station are also faintly Italianate.

The Great Northern gloried in its reticence. London stock brick is used throughout; you can see the beginning of it in the Station Hotel at Peterborough. London stock brick produced magnificent train sheds and buildings like the part of the goods yard called the Granary, in Maiden Lane. The interior of the train sheds in Kings Cross terminus are best of all. Now that the side walls have been cleared of advertisements, the brick arches between the arrival and departure sheds, the iron girders which support the curved roofs, the buttressed side walls and the long platforms have a grandeur that turns the place into a brick, glass and iron cathedral. When it was opened, Kings Cross was the biggest station in England. Its splendour of scale is best appreciated by walking down the departure platform. Trivial and silly seems a garish little bar called the Ridings,

with leather seats, subdued light and piped music interrupted by the station announcer. This little gem is for 'executives'. Next door is a humbler but larger cafeteria for non-executives, which is of course much nicer. The remote waiting room at the end of the platform nearest Scotland seems to have been cleared of the meths drinkers who frequented it.

For all its simplicity, Kings Cross Station was not very practical. Soon two platforms had to be created down the middle between the two sheds. These are narrow and inconvenient. And then when the suburban traffic grew, carrying citizens to stock-brick avenues and station roads in Hornsey, Crouch End, Harringay and out as far as Finchley and Barnet, a little suburban station was built in 1875, alongside the west wall of the train shed. This terminus is still there with two platforms beyond it, added later. It has its own brown refreshment room and bookstall. Platform 17 must be the most old-fashioned and quiet part of any terminus in London, always excepting Marylebone. It is of wood and it does not seem to be used except at rush hours.

The best view of Kings Cross is obtained from another romantic accretion to the original terminus. This is York Road station, "change for Kings Cross main line". It is a down platform only, and the trains disappear down a tunnel to the Metropolitan Underground railway and on by mysterious uneven lines to the City. Sometimes goods trains used it to cross the Thames at Blackfriars. York Road station has what was once a waiting room, and it has a station yard filled with willow herb and a few parked cars belonging to knowing executives who have found their way to its remoteness. From the platform of York Road you see the fine curved roofs of the train sheds, the waiting diesels, the tunnel entrances immediately to your right, and beyond the muddle of the suburban station, the great roof of St Pancras and the Midland red brick contrasting with the brown, smoke-blackened Great Northern brick. Crowning all are the towers and spires of Sir Gilbert Scott's St Pancras Hotel. The romance of Gothic and the romance of engineering are side by side here among the gas-holders of Battle Bridge, and the shiny cobbled lorry routes which cross it.

Of the appalling complications of Kings Cross Underground station, it is needless for me to give much description, since no-one in their senses would use the place if he could help it. The Metropolitan Railway which connects Kings Cross with the City and Paddington, was the first Underground in the world, and was opened in 1863. It must now be the slowest and worst, despite electrification. The tube railways, that is to say those approached by lifts and escalators, are now threefold at Kings Cross.

To get from one Underground station to another in the bowels of the earth is complicated enough, but it is not so complicated as it is to find one's way immediately below the surface by smelly passages to different parts of Kings Cross and different parts of St Pancras. Puzzling notices abound. These passages are naturally filled with bewildered foreigners and poor whites carrying luggage. The headquarters of taxi-land is however at Kings Cross, in York Way. Ever since that station was built it has, with its covered ways, been convenient for Hackney carriages and their successors.

In the 1930s we were all told to admire Kings Cross for its functional simplicity, an earnest of the new dawn. We were told to despise St Pancras for its fussiness though we were allowed to admire the engineer's roof. All the same I have an idea that St Pancras is the more practical station.

Barrows, a passenger and a porter wait for a departure on Platform 8.

LIVERPOOL STREET is the most picturesque and interesting of the London Termini. It has the most varied users. Blond, blue eyed and large, in strangely-cut clothes, to our way of looking at things, the Scandinavians and Dutch arrive from Harwich on the boat train. A few Belgians and French who come by air to Southend airport get in at the nearest Essex station, which is on the less pleasant of the two routes to London, from that bracing estuary resort. The county families, farmers, vicars and agricultural manufacturers come in from Norfolk, East Suffolk and outer Essex, from the Gainsborough, Crome and Constable landscapes of flint church towers, deep red brick manor houses, willows, elms, malt houses and mills. The ladies often travel second class; most of the men go first, except of course the vicars. Finally there is the huge commuter traffic, once far the biggest in London, from those brick two-storey and bay-windowed boxes that stretch over the flat fields of the unfashionable villages of the Lea Valley. An official of the hotel told me that Liverpool Street made him think of a great dragon, belching out at breakfast time thousands of people, and in pre-diesel days, smoke as well, and drawing them in again with their white, exhausted faces, after tea.

Just as the old parish churches of England are the gradual growth of many centuries, so are large railway stations; though a gradual growth of the last century and a bit. Liverpool Street is the most interesting example, and rewards the railway antiquarian with startling features. The Eastern Counties Railway had a station at Shoreditch in the 1840s. 'It is a long straggling block of warehouses, with nothing more striking about it than the clock in the centre, and the wide yard facing the Standard Theatre.' So 'that most unfortunate of lines' is described in Routledge's Guide to London of 1862. Then it merged with other companies like the Eastern Union, and pushed forward into the City, which it reached in February 1874. St Pancras had been built in 1868 in a magnificent and sumptuous Gothic style, so far as the hotel was concerned. The Great Eastern Railway, as these eastern lines were now re-named, was not to be outdone. It too went Gothic and employed E. Wilson, a civil engineer of the days when architecture and civil engineering were less divided, to build the new offices and carriage entrance, and what may well have been the first part of the hotel, in a simplified early English style, in East Anglian yellow brick with stone mouldings for the lancet windows, plate tracery and attached columns. The carriage entrances to this splendid affair were marked by a row of six Gothic Portland stone plinths for elaborate iron gas lamp standards. One survives, plinth only. The roofs and gables of the offices were topped with iron-work and the tower down at the station end had a tiled spire with much iron-work. The parsimony and arrogance of the old-fashioned with-it architects who still dominated British Railways, removed most of the ironwork and did not repair the spire after war-damage.

The large many-styled Great Eastern Hotel is on a hill above the station, and approached at various levels, by foot and road. It is the only hotel in the City and a very good one, especially for lunch. By great good fortune it has been spared 'streamlining' and other pseudo simplicities of the early 1950s, and has been redecorated in a sympathetic style. It is so much part of the station and its architecture and history, that it is the best way to approach the architecture of the whole. On Liverpool Street you see the three stages of this bit of railway development; first the Early English brick and stone of the Great Eastern Terminus, then a later phase, the hotel. It is in a vaguely Renaissance style and has a glass-domed restaurant with dancing sylphs of 1903, painted by Ingham Bell. The staircase of this part of the hotel is impressive, with Louis-Seize style ironwork, but Italianate plasterwork, and the name Maples is suggested in much of the furniture. On to this 1884 hotel was added in 1901, an Anglo-French Renaissance building designed by Colonel Robert Edis (he was a volunteer colonel of the 1890s, who sometimes wore his uniform in the office, and was used by Edward VII to design the ballroom at Sandringham, and by Sir Blundell Maple for the Great Central's terra cotta hotel on the Marylebone Road). Externally, this part of the building on both the Liverpool Street and Bishopsgate fronts badly needs a clean. The prevailing colours will be found to be white stone and red brick. Inside there are really splendid rooms, some done by the Colonel in Louis-Seize style and used for banquets, others slightly Elizabethan. There is much marble and brass and there are two Masonic temples, one Grecian and very splendiferous, the other Egyptian and slightly less so. This whole semi-Masonic block is called the Abercorn Rooms.

And now let us go out into Bishopsgate and turn into the newer part of the station, which was added in 1894 and serves the Southend and South Essex part of the line. Its architect was W. N. Ashbee, head of the G.E.R. architectural department, who designed Norwich (Thorpe), Colchester, Hertford, Felixstowe, Southend (Victoria) and Wolferton stations. It is of red brick and vaguely Dutch in style to remind one of Miss Hook of Holland and the Harwich boats. In moulded brick *in tympana* cherubs are sculpted, acting as porters, surveyors and signalmen. The grand prospect is when you look east and see the vast iron roofs of this new part of the station. You find yourself on an elevated walk, a long and attractive one, very different from the windy, empty 'podium' of

Right Steam's Cathedral. The piers of the double aisle missing the fern fronds that originally adorned them.

Opposite Home from work to semi-rural Essex, 5.50pm on the East Side.

the new Barbican, and the walk takes you past the white wooden Stationmaster's Office, which looks about 1910 in date, and was a tea shop in the Edwardian baroque style one associates with the early days of Fuller's. It also has some rather Scottish-looking art-nouveau stained glass, heavily leaded and pretty.

This high walk all under the roof of the station takes you past the original English yellow brick-and-stone Gothic of the Great Eastern's first effort, into the really splendid vista of columns and iron roofs of what most people mean by Liverpool Street Station. The Great Eastern wanted their train shed to be Cathedral-like as well as the buildings, and the effect is indeed Cathedral-like. Double columns support the two main aisles. Beyond these are yet further aisles. The eastward view is enlivened by a delightful verandah fret, outlined black against the grey east London sky. Unfortunately the capitals of the columns which support this quadruple roof were stripped of their ironwork leaves after the war – some false economy measure – but perforated iron brackets remain.

Opposite Liverpool Street nocturnes – the silence of the night.

Above The erstwhile teahouse perched in the air as the stationmaster's office.

Left Suburban traffic, early morning rush.

On the buildings and in different parts of the station the magic letters G.E.R. survive. By some great good fortune a sister teashop to what is now the Stationmaster's Office remains perched on our upland walk. I know no greater pleasure for elevenses in London than to sit in this teaplace and watch the trains arrive and depart. Later the crowds are too great.

Once you are on the ground floor of either Liverpool Street Station, you are entirely lost.

Nowhere in London is there quite so bad a connection with the Underground. But while you are looking for it you may come into the main booking hall, which was needlessly converted internally into two storeys, 1950s 'Contemporary' style. Here the Great Eastern War Memorial remains, a chaste and large classic marble affair of 1920. It was on returning from the unveiling of this that Sir Henry Wilson was shot on his way to his horse in Eaton Square.

Opposite 'I know of no greater pleasure for elevenses in London than to sit in this teaplace'.

Left A glimpse through plate tracery, East Side, from the footbridge.

I HAVE KNOWN this delightful hidden old terminus since boyhood. I first found it when trying to get into a forgotten and long-demolished parish church, St Catherine Coleman. The church was permanently locked. When I eventually found a churchwarden who reluctantly accompanied me with the key, it was worth the trouble – box pews, galleries, carved altarpiece and pulpit and clear glass. Unsuccessful visits to the churchwarden in the past had taken me towards the homely front of the station. Some trees in the churchyard of demolished St Catherine's mark one entrance to the station. Railway Place is another.

In those days with a half crown in my pocket and baulked of getting into the church, I went up the broad stairs on the west side of the station and sampled the London and Blackwall railway which ran trains quite empty, every fifteen minutes above the east London chimney pots past soaring white Hawksmoor churches to a forgotten and palatial terminus on a quay, where the river is so broad that the journey was like one ending on the sea-shore. Blackwall Station was an Italian palace in stockbrick with stone dressings and designed by Sir William Tite in 1840. The London & Blackwall Railway founded in 1836 was the first to penetrate the sacred walls of the City of London. It was built to compete with the river traffic of the Thames. People living in Woolwich and across the Thames at Gravesend could reach the City sooner, it was hoped. The hopes were not fully realised. I remember the delightful old-fashioned rolling stock and once travelled on it first class, where the seats were cushions of black leather with buttons, and the carriage door had so rarely been opened that the compartment smelt and felt like the interior of a family brougham left forgotten in the stables.

The booking hall for Tilbury and Southend.

The outer end of the
station seen from the
steps of Crutched Friars
House – an eighteenth
century mansion which the
railways spared. The
Crutched Friars, so named
from the cross they carried
on a staff, settled here in
the parish of St Olave at
the end of the 13th
century.

The Blackwall Railway and the Eastern Counties Railway (later the Great Eastern) promoted a more ambitious line than the first attempt to steal the traffic from Thames steamers and barges. They built the London, Tilbury and Southend Railway, which could mop up tons of river traffic from Tilbury Docks, and eventually holiday traffic from Southend. Southend became the poor man's Brighton. It must have been from Fenchurch Street that Charlie Chaplin set out with his mother and brother in the 1890s, and could not believe the wall of blue which he saw at the end of Southend High Street, and which turned out to be the sea. Of course the London, Tilbury and Southend Railway was a bigger affair than the London & Blackwall, so it had to have a London station. The original terminus of the London & Blackwall was in the Minories. The same line built Fenchurch Street station in

Ornate stairs lead heart and eye up to the spacious terminus, all on the first floor.

Opposite A largely untouched Victorian railway terminus basks in summer sun. Who's for Southend-on-Sea?

1853 as we see it today, and this station also served the newcomer, the LT&S. The London to Blackwall trains used to leave from No. 1 platform on the right hand side as you went in, the trains for Tilbury and the Great Eastern Railway left from the other platforms. One casualty of this enlarged line was the Mill Yard Seventh Day Baptist chapel and school belonging to a rare Cromwellian sect now only surviving in America.

The station has been less messed about than any London terminus. Bombs, if there were any, have done damage which is reparable. Only the London to Blackwall offices eastward of the station façade have disappeared. Mr Alan Jackson tells us how the Great Eastern took over the London and Blackwall in 1862 on a 999-year lease, with a rent equal to 4½ per cent of the Company's ordinary capital. 'It was shortly after this that the sinecurist Blackwall directors felt able to give up their board room to the first-class ladies. They did, however, continue to meet elsewhere twice a year until the 1923 grouping, to receive their guaranteed rent and declare a dividend, and then, weakened by these exertions, to dine and wine together'.

George Berkeley, the engineer of the LT&S, designed the station and its façade which reflects the structure of the interior. It was built 1853–1854 in the days when engineers did not mind turning their hands to architecture, and produced such notable buildings as The Albert Hall and the tunnels and bridges and viaducts of the Great Western. In its modest way Fenchurch Street station is a good example of the engineer-architect tradition. Its façade is of grey stockbrick with stone adornments. The entrance front at street level is low and rusticated with alternate windows and doors. There was originally a flat canopy above this, but it was replaced in the 1860s by a zig-zag canopy, which besides being efficient, has fairground charm. The main façade is that at first floor level which consists of eleven round-arched windows with pilasters between them. Above these is a frieze surmounted by a crescent-shaped pediment in the middle of which is the station clock. The booking hall is at street level, and stairs with attractive cast-iron railings mount either side of the booking hall to the main concourse, on the first floor. The

railway is carried from East London into the station over brick arches, and the concourse was originally lighted by the large round-arched windows on the façade. The train shed has a crescent-shaped trussed roof of iron, from which descend charming things like flying saucers which hold fluorescent lights. The walls of the station are stockbrick with arches and a good many advertisements. There are only four platforms and these are very crowded at rush hours with commuters from Southend and Shoeburyness and Tilbury. The line is also a quicker route to the City from Dagenham and Upminster than the District railway, which has so many more stops.

On the concourse is a refreshment room built in the moderne style of the 1930s, with prevailing colours of brown and cream. The platforms have been lengthened beyond the train shed, so that there is an exit at the far end of the station into John Street, now named Crosswall. Here is an Italianate building of three storeys which was once the offices of the LT&SR. Fenchurch Street has no close connection with the Underground. The nearest Underground station, Tower Hill, is several minutes' walk, and none too easy to find, unless you know the City well. The forecourt in front of the station is one of the only places in the City of London where there is sometimes a waiting taxi cab.

Fenchurch Street offers quite the most enjoyable expedition from London between mid-day and tea-time. A day-return to Southend (Central) carries one in fifty minutes by a fast train, first through the remains of East London with its old houses and new inhuman tower blocks of flats and distant views of shipping and steeples, past the windmill at Upminster and out into unspoiled country, with flint churches and wide fields and, in the distance, the shores of Kent and far-off oil refineries. The ruins of Hadleigh Castle, which Constable painted, are on your left, and then there are the whelk stalls and weather-boarded houses of Leigh-on-Sea, and finally Southend. Downhill to the High Street and a tram ride along the pier for a mile and a third to a good restaurant and views of the great ships waiting to come in at the Nore, and air like wine and sky and water everywhere.

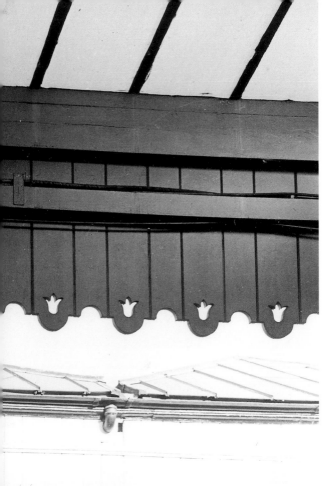

LONDON BRIDGE station was for the first London railway. It was opened in 1836 and ran to Greenwich over brick arches. Its first terminus was in Spa Road, Bermondsey, where some fluted Doric columns of cast-iron survive. In December of that year the Lord Mayor of London and the Corporation, which must have included that inexplicable figure, 'the Secondary and High Baliff of Southwark,' welcomed the first steam train into London at the new terminus on the Surrey bank of the Thames. Thus London Bridge is the oldest railway terminus in London, and it certainly looks it. It is a terminus to which few Continental passengers now come, and at which few Americans must have alighted from the other side of the Atlantic. London Bridge is indeed the most complicated, muddled and unwelcoming of all London termini. Its platforms are narrow and draughty, it seems to be several stations in one, and they are connected by toilsome footbridges and mysterious underground passages. At the time of writing, the new London Bridge over the Thames – the third in succession of those which have crossed the Thames since Saxon times – is being built.

The London, Brighton &
South Coast Railway's City
terminus.

London Bridge is symbolic of the City of
London to which it is the south-eastern, and
was for long, the chief entrance. The City is a
mysterious place of alleys and short cuts,
hidden cafes, underground passages, and blind
corners. So is London Bridge station, but it
lacks the churches and Livery Company Halls,
which make the City different from the rest of
London. Instead it has a Cathedral, Southwark
Cathedral, which is buried among its railway
lines. Here Gower, the poetical friend of
Chaucer, is interred, along with the predeces-
sors of such well known Americans as Ralph
Waldo Emerson and John Harvard. The La
Farge window to the last named (1905) is not to
be missed, nor is the marble tomb to Lancelot
Andrews. The noble nave is late Victorian. In
fact Southwark Cathedral, long overshadowed
by London Bridge station is now being
swamped by formidable office blocks being
erected in the 1950s style, on the approaches to
the station.

London Bridge station symbolises the City in
another way. It is secret. I do not see how any-
one of the thousands a day who have to use it
during rush hours, can find his way about without a long apprenticeship. This is the place to
hint at the importance of that powerful village
of which this is the first railway station. The
City too is secret. It is run by only a few thou-
sand people, one might almost say only a few
hundred, and they all know each other more or
less, or at any rate they know of each other. In
the City, if a man gives his word to a bargain,
it is honoured. Americans say 'but where is
your attorney? Why is there no contract to
sign? How do I know what you have said will
be done?' The truth is that if a citizen of London does not honour his word the rumour goes
round the village and he is politely ostracised.
Most of the business of the City is done by
conversation and calling in at offices. It is also
done in Exchanges and Streets. Of course it
is increasingly done over the telephone. Once
business has stopped, then the conversation
changes. Among the top people it changes to
shooting, salmon fishing, yachting and
hunting, and slightly further down the scale
it turns to golf, tennis and rugby football and
so on until it reaches League football and the
Pools.

Joyous undisciplined
ornamentation running
through the station.

40

After London Bridge was opened to Deptford in 1836 and to Greenwich in 1838, the London Bridge to Croydon line was completed. This was followed by the South Eastern Railway, and the London, Brighton and South Coast Railway, all converging on brick arches high above. The overcrowding was such that one line crossed the river into Cannon Street in 1866, stopping at London Bridge on the way. Another crossed to Charing Cross in 1864, and in the same year yet one more crossed to Blackfriars. All these different rival lines were renamed the Southern Railway in 1923 and all are now electrified. Today London Bridge copes at peak hours with more thousands of passengers than it can conveniently hold.

To look at the station in the middle of the day, as I have done, one could scarcely believe the misery its lack of accommodation, its narrow platforms and steep heart-testing steps, have caused millions of Londoners for the last hundred years. T. S. Eliot sums them up, those thousands who cross from London Bridge to the City, in the opening section of 'The Waste Land' (1922).

> Unreal City,
> Under the brown fog of a winter dawn,
> A crowd flowed over London Bridge, so many,
> I had not thought death had undone so many.
> Sighs, short and infrequent, were exhaled,
> And each man fixed his eyes before his feet.
> Flowed up the hill and down King William Street,
> To where Saint Mary Woolnoth kept the hours
> With a dead sound on the final stroke of nine.

Eliot was a clerk at Lloyds Bank in the City when he wrote those lines. London Bridge was a station at which clerks, secretaries and at earlier times of the morning, office cleaners arrived. Directors and Company Chairmen would come much later, and few would get out at London Bridge, unless they had estates in Kent. The two chief termini for Directors and Chairman in the City of London, are Waterloo leading to the conifers of Surrey, and good shooting country in Hampshire, and Liverpool Street where the Bankers and Brewers go to their large houses in Norfolk and Suffolk. Blackfriars, Holborn Viaduct and Fenchurch Street, like Broad Street, are for clerical workers.

A typical entrance out of rush hour. A non-commuter.

London Bridge station has few remains of its architectural glory. The South Eastern Railway built an Italianate frontage of brick faced with stucco in 1851, this was designed by Samuel Beazley, but the London, Brighton and South Coast Railway's rather handsome terminus survives on the south side of this station, at any rate so far as its barrel-shaped cast-iron roof is concerned, with its central arch over platforms 15 to 18, supported on fluted columns and with elaborate spandrels and lattice girders. Most of the station was heavily bombed by the Germans in the last war, and has been hardly repaired at all. Here and there, as you enter on the London and Brighton side, you

Approaches to London
Bridge station carried over
brick arches.

may see a fluted Doric column in cast-iron, and
in a particularly dingy waiting room there is a
column with an Egyptian lotus leaf capital,
surviving from some forgotten grandeur. At
the time of writing, the station is, as it always
was, a collection of bewildering signs, book-
stalls, brown and uninviting bars, shops, one of
which is surprisingly called 'The Hosiery and
Underwear Bar,' as though one could drink
such delicious things, and steps and passages
to one or other of the twenty-two platforms. A
forbidding earnest of the future is a tall 'point

block' of about fifteen or twenty storeys, just
erected and quite empty. It stands where a
pleasant curved Crescent approached the station from the Borough High Street. At its feet
is an entrance to the Underground station.

Outside the main station at the southern end
of London Bridge and next to the handsome
Hibernia Chambers (1849) is the Bridge House
Hotel (1839). It was erected by the Hay's Wharf
Company and must be the first railway hotel in
the world. It is in a classic style and of Portland
stone. The top floor or Belvedere which surveys

the Thames, has a rich plaster ceiling with semi-domes and mirrors with angels. The architecture could be by Decimus Burton or Samuel Beazley. A foretaste of the grandeur of the Belvedere, is the pillared entrance hall on the ground floor.

In Edwardian times, City men, many of the Lord Mayors and Aldermen and Common Councillors, lived on the salubrious heights of Streatham and Lewisham and the Crystal Palace. They had detached residences, with carriage drive and private gas lamps above speckled laurels. These were the merchant's first taste of country life after his forebear's cramped living premises over the place of business in the City. Possibly it is the inconvenience and discomfort of London Bridge station, as much as the popularity of the motor car, that has driven the prosperous City merchant of today far out into Surrey and Sussex and even north of the Thames into Buckinghamshire and the Cotswolds.

The LB&SCR train shed as seen on arrival.

THESE SAD TERMINI are an expression of blighted hopes. Steam traction was going to link London with the Continent. The Crystal Palace, re-erected on Sydenham Hill, was going to beckon those north of the Thames in their thousands to the Surrey heights. Already elegant villas of brick and stone had risen, yellow, grey and white, Italianate, Gothic and Swiss, each in its own garden in the neighbourhood of the Crystal Palace. Steam trains, instead of pausing reverently outside the capital in Lambeth marshes, or by the Borough High Street, had dared to cross the river, and invade not just Pimlico and Trafalgar Square but the City of London itself – Grosvenor Bridge 1860, Charing Cross 1864, Cannon Street 1866, Blackfriars 1864.

What hopes there were! At the termini gigantic hotels, gabled and turreted, were to entertain foreigners, after their channel crossing, and English businessmen with their families, pausing for a night in London on their way to Nice or St Petersburg. Three of these gigantic hotels were built at Cannon Street, Holborn Viaduct and Charing Cross. None remains but that at Charing Cross.

The hotel was designed on its southern side to fit in with the curved roof of the terminus. This roof is now lowered. Still more successful, as architecture, was the Cannon Street Hotel, even vaster than that at Charing Cross, and it too was designed by E. M. Barry. For most of the present century, until its destruction since the war, the hotel was used as offices and had rooms for mysterious public meetings. I remember opening the door of one to find the Upper Ouse Catchment Board sitting round a green baize table. Cannon Street's nobility is only preserved in the stone towers by E. M. Barry, with their hollow brick arches and leaded cupolas and spires above, and the immense stock-brick walls of what once was the train shed. The towers fitted in well with Wren's steeples in the City as they were designed to do. Now most of Wren's steeples are hidden by dull office blocks, erected in the last twenty years.

Cannon Street station was built, together with its hotel, in 1865–1867. The cast-iron roof supported on brick walls exactly fitted the design of the train shed side of the hotel. Its

engineer was Sir John Hawkshaw. Cannon Street train shed like that of Charing Cross was roofed without internal supports, and until St Pancras station roof was completed in 1868, they must have been the largest roofs of their kind. Cannon Street was built by the South Eastern Railway, and Holborn Viaduct by the London, Chatham and Dover Railway. These railway subsequently merged as the South Eastern and Chatham, and were the combined deadly enemies of the London, Brighton and South Coast Railway, whose headquarters were at London Bridge.

Of these stations the one that remains comparatively unmutilated is that which is now called Blackfriars. Surprisingly enough the District railway station, on its western side, facing all travellers who come to the City along the Embankment, is Turkish. Sadly it is now a Turkish ruin, for only the ground and part of the first floors remain. It is of grey stock brick and the ornament is in crisply carved Portland stone. It was originally a three-storey building, flanked with towers and minarets. It was built in 1870. I suppose the eastern style must have been adopted because

Opposite Across the Thames from Cannon Street.

Above Cannon Street desolation.

Looking south between Blackfriars Bridge (right) and the railway bridges (left) from the Middlesex bank.

it was the temporary eastern terminus of the rather uninteresting District Railway which brought Ealing, Richmond and Wimbledon to London, and which was the rival of the Metropolitan. Next to this station and connected with it by some dingy wooden stairs is St Paul's terminus of the London, Chatham and Dover Railway, now renamed Blackfriars. Between the Turkish façade of the District Railway – and it was only recently I discovered from Sir

John Summerson for certain that the architect of this remarkable building was F. J. Ward, because in those days architects and engineers were not consciously separate professions – there runs an offensive bridge carrying the London, Chatham and Dover Railway to the now demolished station at Ludgate Hill, and across that hill itself, where it defaces the view of St Paul's with Southern Railway moderne pseudo simplicity on its way to Holborn

Viaduct and King's Cross. Facing Queen Victoria Street and the offices of the *Times* newspaper, is the London Chatham and Dover's answer to the District terminus. It is red instead of grey, and Italianate instead of Turkish, and it too has flanking towers. The style is Italian, no doubt to give a European touch to the passer-by. Cut into the heavily rusticated brick pilasters, which adorn this façade, are the names of the principal stations reached by the SE and CR – Baden-Baden and Beckenham, Bremen and Broadstairs, Brindisi and Bromley, Ramsgate and Leipzig, Sittingbourne and Marseilles, Westgate-on-Sea and St Petersburg, they flank the entrances with bewildering supplication unnoticed by the sad commuters hurrying to queue on the echoing woodwork of the booking hall floor. It was in this booking hall that I asked for a return to St Petersburg and was referred to Victoria Continental.

Above left The London, Chatham & Dover railway bridge abutment.

Above right Engravings from better times.

WATERLOO is 'one of the really great stations of the world.' So says O. S. Nock in his informative history of the London and South Western Railway. The personality of that railway still pervades the station. It is associated with fast electric trains taking executives to the coniferous half-world of Woking, with soldiers going to the slippery heather and rhododendrons of Aldershot and with schoolboys and mental patients being drafted off to large institutions on sandy soil. It has twenty-one platforms ranged in a crescent facing west. It is a much older station than it looks and came into importance when Southampton took precedence over Portsmouth and Dover as a safe harbour for Channel shipping and eventually for large America-bound liners. The London and Southampton Railway was thought of in 1831 and reached London in 1838 with a handsome Classic Terminus by Sir William Tite at Nine Elms which has lately been demolished. The line also served Portsmouth and Basingstoke and passengers wanted to be taken nearer London than the remote Lambeth Marsh where Nine Elms stood.

By 1848 this railway, now known as the London and South Western, came over brick arches to the foot of Waterloo Bridge. To begin with Waterloo Bridge was the name of the station. He needs to be an industrious industrial archaeologist indeed who would trace any surviving bricks and stones of the original station. Across the Waterloo Road in a street north of the Union Jack Club is the original entrance to that mysterious station – Waterloo Junction put up by the S.E.R. in civil engineer's Lombardic style of 1869. It was once connected with the main Waterloo by rail but now only wooden passages carry one over the chimney pots to its echoing draughty platforms. Down in the parcels station of Waterloo itself on the Waterloo Road side there are a few yellow brick walls with red brick, classic mouldings surviving from the south part of Waterloo built in 1878. Over the northern platforms, that is to say Nos 16 to 21, the spandrels of the cast-iron columns supporting the glass roof date from 1885 when the north station was added.

What survives from the earlier Waterloo stations is the arrangement of the roofs which is different from that of any other London terminus. It is not elegant, nor is it offensive. It is practical and the main part was rebuilt 1901–1922. Even in the days of steam Waterloo was not as sooty and black as other stations. Over the concourse, where canned music is meant to alleviate the stress of rush hours, the roofs jut out at right angles from the main building, but over the twenty-one platforms they are ranged horizontally on a forest of columns best seen from the cocktail bar of the Surrey Dining Room. Over the north station the roof is the original of 1885.

The Surrey Dining Room – the very name conjures up the new hygienic picture the London and South Western painted of itself in the days when Sir Herbert Walker was general manager from 1912–1937 and when A. W. Szlumper was chief engineer. Both these great men wore moustaches and rimless spectacles. They electrified the line and eventually the whole of what became the Southern Railway's suburban system. Sir Herbert would have no truck with the London Underground system and was determined to stop it crossing the Thames any more. He even had his own underground railway known as 'The Drain' which still runs from a bleak, white tiled station at Waterloo its undulating length under the Thames to the Bank where its pleasant smell of a changing room after games gives way to the anonymous breath of London Transport as one ascends by moving pavements towards the street.

Right Time suspended between rusticated stone and tempered steel.

Right Sturdy steel supports in the Edwardian part of the station.

Opposite The warp and woof of roofs and platforms.

The other thing that is different about Waterloo is its architecture which is, Dr Pevsner's Guide informs me, by an architect named J. R. Scott. If it is all by the same hand he grew more exuberant in his style with the years. The Booking Hall – alas no more – at which one arrived after ascending that long snake of a slope from Lambeth marsh to the level of the platform was in a restrained Edwardian style of 1911. Coupled Roman-Doric columns of marble supported a plain coved ceiling. It was impressive and simple and as though influ-

enced by Piranesi. The iron work alone was elaborate. As seems always to happen when British Railways have been left a handsome bit of architecture, it became cluttered with wooden benches suitable for a tennis club and drab tin lockers for luggage ranged with no regard for the space they occupy. In 1971 the architects of British Railways finally destroyed it. This pre-1914 part of the new station also contains the Surrey Dining Room. It is approached by marble stairs and by lift. Coupled columns support the staircase ceiling.

Niches adorn its walls. The dining room itself is a spacious, quiet room panelled in Georgian style in English oak. It twinkles with light from leaded windows looking over the station and the approach road.

'Belgium, Italy, Dardanelles, France, Mesopotamia, Egypt, North Sea.' These names are carved in stone over the Victory arch which was opened by Queen Mary in 1922 and which was the last great gesture of the London and South Western Railway which then sank into the Southern Region. Clearly Mr Scott when he designed this great entrance to the new Waterloo after the 1914 War was determined to outdo Sir Ralph Knott's enormous County Hall on the Thames only a few yards away. He had had a look at Piranesi, the etchings of Brangwyn and Muirhead Bone and the rich Edwardian baroque of provincial Town Halls. As he has executed his design in Portland stone and bronze, it suddenly stands out as splendid and generous now that an anonymous slab of office building designed by what one can only take to be a computer has been built alongside it.

The Victory Arch prepared one for the great splendours Waterloo had yet to show. These were the Long Bar outside which appeared the words 'Refreshment Buffet' in white art-nouveau lettering on blue mosaics. Inside the style was rich baroque from which not even modern bar fittings could remove the glamour. The walls were green, white and grey marble, the columns were marble and fluted and with elaborate capitals. But this Long Bar was coarse compared with the Windsor Bar which still survives opposite Platforms 16 to 21 and nearly next to the Victory Arch. Here is Edwardian de luxe style at its most refined. The prevailing colours are grey and white. These should be lit, and no doubt once were, by bronze electroliers with cut glass shades. As it is, the Ionic columns and fluted pilasters, the mirrors and marble, the domed pay boxes with curved glass such as one saw in early cinemas, all suggest a richer age. They are de luxe, remembered as late as 1922.

The sad thing about Waterloo is that road engineers seem utterly to have ignored it and devised the most circuitous routes possible to approach it. None of these allow one to see its architecture. Very few people use the steps

under the Victory Arch. They can only cross the road to look up at it at the risk of their lives. The style in which this practical airy station is built may be temporarily unfashionable. To me it looks far less dated than the Southern Railway-Moderne News cinema of the 1930s which was squashed in along the concourse wall by platform 1.

Opposite Traceried entrance to the luggage hall from the taxi road.

Above Domed pay-boxes of the Windsor Bar. Edwardian de Luxe at its most refined.

CHARING CROSS was opened in 1864, and the railway bridge across to it was started in 1860. The station was, because of its location near Trafalgar Square, the most illustrious in London. Its fortunes have risen and fallen with those of the Strand, at whose western end the station stands. The broad Strand joins the City of London, where they make the money, to the west end of London, where they spend it. Those pepper-pot domes on the stucco triangle of shops nearly facing the station, were a prelude to the departed stucco glories of Regent Street, out of sight and west of Trafalgar Square. The north side of the Strand had a rather fast reputation in Victorian times – Romano's Restaurant, from whose entrance you could see the clock on the Law courts; the cigar divans in one of which Mr Harding from Barchester paused to smoke a cigar; on the river side were the Savoy Hotel, and, in those days smarter than the Savoy, the Cecil Hotel, of which Arnold Bennett wrote. There was a Punch joke about it, showing a lady in a front seat of an open top horsebus, saying to the driver "Do you stop at the Cecil?" and his reply "Do I stop at the Cecil, on 28 bob a week?". There was the Tivoli Music Hall and famous music hall songs like 'Let's all go down the Strand' sung by Charles Whittle; Ella Shields sang

I'm Burlington Bertie I rise at 10.30
And saunter along like a toff,
I walk down the Strand with my gloves
on each hand,
And I walk back again with them off.

All the great hotels were here, the Metropole and the Victoria in Northumberland Avenue, the Grand and Morley's and Charing Cross Station Hotel itself, in the French Renaissance style, with its 250 bedrooms, opened in 1865 and designed by Edward Middleton Barry, the son of the architect of the Houses of Parliament. It was from Charing Cross sometimes that Sherlock Holmes, whose exploits featured in the Strand Magazine, left in pursuit of criminals in South London and on the Continent. In the Northumberland Hotel, on the site of Northumberland House, Sir Henry Baskerville, the Baronet, came to stay, and left his new tan boots which he had bought in the Strand out-

side his bedroom door, and one of them was
stolen. Charing Cross Station was the gateway
to Paris and the Continent, those notorious
areas of immorality. Even the concourse of
Charing Cross Station under its great semi-
circular roof of glass, has a slightly immoral
reputation. A. H. Binstead, 'Pitcher' of the
'Pink'un' quoted in 1903

> The terminus of Charing Cross
> Is haunted when it rains
> By Nymphs, who there a shelter seek
> And wait for mythic trains.

The general foreignness of the station was
emphasised by the Bureau de Change in a shop
on the cobbled forecourt, and an exotic tobac-
conist's on the other. Standing in the middle of
the red granite concourse among the taxi cabs
rises the Eleanor Cross designed by Edward
Middleton Barry in 1865. Its crisply carved
Portland stone figures and pinnacles, and its
red mansfield stone panels, are so smeared
with pigeon droppings, that many people think
it is as old as the time of Edward the First,
whose Queen it commemorates. The diversified
Mansard roofs of the hotel were mercilessly
demolished after bomb damage in the war,
and the top storeys are now a weak parody of
Georgian, an insult both to the bold coarse
Victorian Renaissance below them, and the
skyline of this prominent part of London.

The station is the only London terminus to

58

have a cobbled street running under its whole length and very hard it is to find. This street originally went to Hungerford Market, which was down by the banks of the Thames, in the days before the river was embanked and narrowed. The market was somewhat squalid and contained the blacking factory where Dickens worked as a boy. Worn cobbles and uneven kerbstones still recall this once frequented way to market under the station. It leaves from Craven Street and emerges in Villiers Street.

In 1845 a suspension footbridge designed by I. K. Brunel, the railway engineer, crossed from the market to the Surrey bank. When the South Eastern Railway decided to extend its operations from London Bridge to nearer the west end of London, it bought Brunel's suspension bridge and another great railway engineer, Sir John Hawkshaw (1811–1891), brought the line over arches from London Bridge to Charing Cross. The cables of Brunel's footbridge he used to complete Clifton Suspension Bridge which had been designed by Brunel in 1831, but which had not been completed. Hawkshaw's railway bridge to Charing Cross is so severely practical that the late Victorians and Edwardians thought it painfully ugly. It is heavy and straight and carried on fluted pairs of columns. It probably looked better when there was no embankment along the Thames from Westminster to Blackfriars. What the bridge lacked in elegance was made up for by the Charing Cross terminus, whose enormous curved roof nearly one hundred feet above the rails, made the station into a cathedral of brick, glass and iron. Edward Middleton Barry designed the hotel at Charing Cross with Hawkshaw's roof in mind. Thus at the buffer end of the terminus, roof and hotel seemed a single composition, and from the first floor of the hotel, balconies projected to give visitors a view of the trains. But alas on 5th December 1905, at 3.45pm, a dramatic event took place which is so well described by Mr Alan Jackson in his book London's Termini that I quote his own words with his permission:

> . . . there was a sudden and unusual noise. The repair men were seen trying to escape from their precarious situation, and staff and passengers beat a hasty retreat,

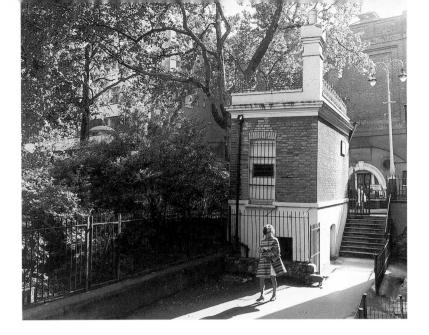

fearing that worse was to follow. It did. Twelve minutes later, the physical strains worked themselves out and 70 ft of the roof, two bays, with the huge windscreen at the river end, crashed down into the station with a roar, pushing the side wall outwards until it tipped over on to the Avenue Theatre at the bottom of Craven Street (now the Playhouse). About 100 men were at work on the reconstruction of that building, and three were crushed to death as the avalanche of iron and bricks thundered through its roof. In the station itself, three more men had died as the 3.50pm train for Hastings was buried in the rubble.

A new roof was constructed but with less regard to the architecture of the hotel. The S and R of SE and CR can be still be seen on the Thames-facing end of the train shed in bold Edwardian style.

An attractive side approach to the station.

Still Dickensian Hungerford Lane.

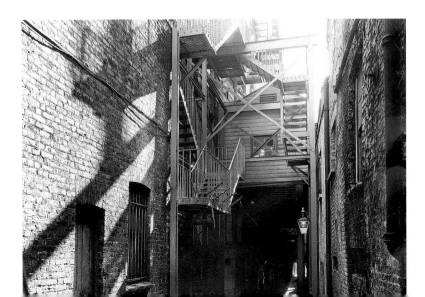

The real splendour of Charing Cross was in the interior of the hotel, and much of this happily remains. There is now no entrance to it from the train shed. The shady ladies and young sparks to whom Charing Cross was the gateway to wickedness on the Continent are dead and Charing Cross has become a commuter's station. Victoria has taken over the Continental trains. But the hotel is so splendid a building that not even British Railways have destroyed it. Its interior is bold Italian Renaissance style, and is entered by a porch under a conservatory at the eastern end of the forecourt. A barrel-vaulted passage leads to the great staircase whose broad carpeted stairs are so inviting that the climb to the first floor where are the principal rooms, seems hardly to be uphill. There on the right down another barrel-vaulted passage is the dining room which, except for that at the Ritz (1906), is the most finely appointed hotel dining room in London. It still retains its corner columns and Renaissance plaster work. Unfortunately the clock which graced one wall and the weather cock which told the direction of the wind on the other, have disappeared. But the room has been redecorated with considerable taste, and so has the lounge which leads to the Conservatory.

During the war this hotel still possessed what my friends and I used to call The Club. Down the main corridor on the station side of the hotel there were a bar and coffee room, whose french windows opened onto the balcony, where one could sit and watch the trains. The smoking room had been refurnished in, I should think, about 1905, with long comfortable leather chairs and benches. There was even a small library with a set of Shakespeare and a set of Scott, and a quiet white-uniformed waiter of pre-1914 type, in charge of things. Alas! this room and a billiard room next to it are no more, and I can only imagine they have been given over to conferences and committee meetings.

The Charing Cross, Euston and Hampstead Electric Underground Railway terminated at Charing Cross in 1907 under the main concourse at a station now called the Strand. Its lift doors and green and white tiled passages are a singularly undefaced relic of pre-1914 Underground style. After the 1914 war this line

was extended to meet the District Railway at Charing Cross Underground station on the Embankment. Here Mr H. W. Ford in 1913 had designed a handsome Classic station with a domed booking hall and monumental Portland stone frontage to both Villiers Street and Victoria Embankment, he also provided steps to the Hungerford footbridge. Though all the stations at Charing Cross are now for suburban traffic above and below ground, the terminus still contains a flavour of impending journeys through Surrey and Kent to Folkestone and Dover, whence mail steamers can carry us to Calais, Ostend, Boulogne and even Paris.

Opposite Exit from Charing Cross Station looking down the Strand.

Above The dining room of the Charing Cross Hotel, the best proportioned Victorian hotel dining room in London.

THIS IS London's most conspicuous monument to commercial rivalry. The station buildings at Victoria are a fascinating study. There are three stations here, the least interesting of which is the Underground, which takes in the Inner Circle and District Lines. It is, however, graced on the westbound platform with a public bar. In the last few months this has been shut, owing, I am told, to 'a shortage of staff'. It could of course be that too many people reeled out onto the electric lines, but as there are still bars on the Inner Circle platforms at Liverpool Street and Sloane Square, perhaps this one at Victoria may yet be reprieved. Below this is the new Victoria Line Underground station. It is hygienic and efficient, as is the line itself, and far the fastest and quietest underground in Britain.

The first railway to cross the Thames at this western part of London was the London, Brighton and South Coast Railway and it crossed in 1860. The west end terminus of the London to Brighton line was situated here and a splendid hotel, the Grosvenor, was built to go with it in 1861. It was not the first of the Railway Hotels but it was one of the earliest. It is in an Italianate style, and had most surprising and rich carving on the outside, in Bath stone. The French roofs, Mansard style, with their balls and spikes on the top are a very pleasant addition to the skyline. And inside, despite a certain amount of with-itry in the new colour schemes, the strong architecture still survives. The architect of this handsome and ponderous building was J. T. Knowles, the friend of the poet Tennyson and himself the founder and editor of *The Nineteenth Century*. He also designed some houses in the Grosvenor Hotel style on Clapham Common, and I have an idea he also did some down at Hove.

If you stood between the exit from the Underground station and the bus terminus, and looked across to the muddle of Victoria station (and it is a rather happy sort of muddle), you could see the story of British Railways. The new bus terminus (1971) put up by London Transport blots out the comprehensive view of this interesting collection. On the left facing

Platform One, for the Continent.

Opposite the rich Edwardian Baroque of the South Eastern and Chatham Railway's Continental route to Dover, the ferry and Paris; beyond, the duller Baroque of the London Brighton and South Coast Railway.

Left The original modest London Chatham and Dover Railway frontage round the corner in Hudson's Place.

VICTORIA – THE GATEWAY TO THE CONTINENT

you is the oldest part left, except for the Grosvenor Hotel, of the original Victoria station. This is the terminus of the London, Chatham and Dover Railway, as the South Eastern and Chatham used to be called. It sends trains via Clapham and Peckham Rye (a fine old station) to the other terminus of the South Eastern at London Bridge. It is chiefly known as the Continental part of Victoria Station. The original entrance is round the side, at the east of the whole collection of buildings. It really is a very handsome brick and plaster Roman style building, with three storeys in its main block, a grand booking office, by far the nicest booking office at Victoria, and when you come through the main entrance block onto the platforms, 1 to 8, you see that they are arched over by two elegant curved roofs.

As though faintly aware that this side of Victoria station is a rather good bit of architecture, the Southern Railway had erected a vast sign in inappropriate lettering – GATEWAY TO THE CONTINENT. I doubt if anybody even noticed this lettering because nobody bothers to look at this most handsome side of the station. The South Eastern and Chatham Railway, as it became, which used these platforms 1 to 8 of Victoria, was the deadly rival of its neighbour, the London Brighton and South Coast line. It was probably agents of the London Brighton and South Coast Line which called the London, Chatham and Dover, 'the London Smash 'em and Turnover'. Certainly the South Eastern line had many accidents. But the London, Brighton and South Coast was a very slow and uncomfortable line too, for many years.

Both lines felt inferior to the lines which had Great in front of them, Great Northern, Great Western, Great Central, even the Great Eastern. This South Eastern and Chatham part of Victoria station was built in 1862.

In 1898 the London, Brighton and South Coast Railway decided to redeem its old murky reputation, and to look more up-to-date. So it pulled down its old terminus next to the Grosvenor Hotel and built that red brick Renaissance-style building, with the clock in it. This is the way we come into Victoria when we want to take the train to Brighton and to Sussex. And once inside the booking hall you have a feeling of electrically-lit hygienically Edwardian days. The pillars and the walls are of pale green and white faience. In mosaics over an arch it says 'L.B. and S.C. Ry. Map of Suburban Lines' in art-nouveau lettering. But when you look for the map of the system it is concealed by telephone booths. Not one buffet now survives in this old florid style of the London Brighton and South Coast line. This is sad.

If you want to find that happy character connected with holiday going and the sea, and immoral weekends, well, you find it very much better in the Pullman cars that shake you so much as you go along that splendid one-hour journey to the sea. And I daresay upstairs in this part of Victoria station there are rooms used as offices which still have their art-nouveau decoration. Unfortunately the public parts of the LB and SC side of Victoria have now been done up in Festival simplicity, recalling the priggish days of the 1950s.

The South Eastern and Chatham Railway was determined not to be outdone by the flashy new Renaissance front that the London, Brighton and South Coast had given to its terminus. So alongside its rival in portland stone, it caused A. W. Blomfield to design and build that extraordinary portland stone Baroque terminus. The London, Brighton and South Coast front had maidens carved in stone. Well, the South Eastern and Chatham had even bigger maidens carved in stone on their front. Neither of these fronts look like railway stations, they look more like banks. But they do convey strong individuality and they are a change from the clinical kind of station that gets put up today.

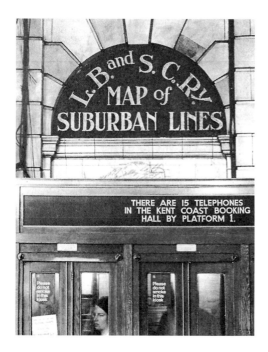

The pleasantly muddled interior of Victoria station must puzzle foreigners. How easily they might find themselves on a Pullman to Brighton instead of on a boat-train to Dover. Victoria station has more notices, more little shops, more bewildering divisions than most of the other London termini. And the people who use it are as varied as the station. In England we think of it chiefly as the station for Brighton. 'Under the Clock at Victoria' is one of the most moving and poetical of William Sansom's short stories. But the clock has now gone to the U.S.A. to decorate a restaurant. Smoking an after-breakfast pipe, the city men come up in the morning from Brighton and Sussex and Surrey. White and defeated in their hundreds they come back to the suburban trains. Set apart on another platform are the fast trains to Brighton. Here are flashier, happier types, longing for the sea air when they leave London, all the better for it when they come back. It is also very much a children's line, this Brighton side of Victoria.

On the Continental side there is quite a different atmosphere. The suburbanites from the Continental side go to less fashionable parts than those on the Brighton side. These parts

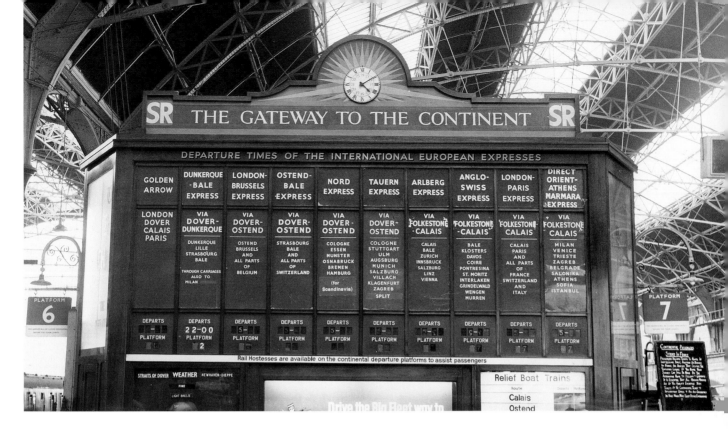

SR THE GATEWAY TO THE CONTINENT SR

DEPARTURE TIMES OF THE INTERNATIONAL EUROPEAN EXPRESSES

GOLDEN ARROW	DUNKERQUE -BALE EXPRESS	LONDON- BRUSSELS EXPRESS	OSTEND- BALE EXPRESS	NORD EXPRESS	TAUERN EXPRESS	ARLBERG EXPRESS	ANGLO- SWISS EXPRESS	LONDON- PARIS EXPRESS	DIRECT ORIENT- ATHENS MARMARA EXPRESS
LONDON DOVER CALAIS PARIS	VIA DOVER- DUNKERQUE	VIA DOVER- OSTEND	VIA DOVER- OSTEND	VIA DOVER- OSTEND	VIA DOVER- OSTEND	VIA FOLKESTONE -CALAIS	VIA FOLKESTONE -CALAIS	VIA FOLKESTONE CALAIS	VIA FOLKESTONE CALAIS
	DUNKERQUE LILLE STRASBOURG BALE THROUGH CARRIAGES ALSO TO MILAN	OSTEND BRUSSELS AND ALL PARTS OF BELGIUM	STRASBOURG BALE AND ALL PARTS OF SWITZERLAND	COLOGNE ESSEN MUNSTER OSNABRUCK BREMEN HAMBURG (for Scandinavia)	COLOGNE STUTTGART ULM AUGSBURG MUNICH SALZBURG VILLACH KLAGENFURT ZAGREB SPLIT	CALAIS BALE ZURICH INNSBRUCK SALZBURG LINZ VIENNA	BALE KLOSTERS DAVOS COIRE PONTRESINA ST. MORITZ INTERLAKEN GRINDELWALD WENGEN MURREN	CALAIS PARIS AND ALL PARTS OF FRANCE SWITZERLAND AND ITALY	MILAN VENICE TRIESTE ZAGREB BELGRADE SALONIKA ATHENS SOFIA ISTANBUL
DEPARTS ■■ PLATFORM	DEPARTS 22-00 PLATFORM 2	DEPARTS 5-■■ PLATFORM	DEPARTS ■■-■■ PLATFORM	DEPARTS ■-■ PLATFORM	DEPARTS ■- PLATFORM	DEPARTS ■-■ PLATFORM	DEPARTS 6-■■ PLATFORM 7	DEPARTS ■-■■ PLATFORM 7	DEPARTS 5-■■ PLATFORM

Rail Hostesses are available on the continental departure platforms to assist passengers

STRAITS OF DOVER **WEATHER** NEWHAVEN-DIEPPE
FINE
LIGHT BREEZE

Relief Boat Trains
Route
Calais
Ostend

will be coming into fashion again soon, the brick houses round the Crystal Palace and in Norwood and Beckenham. High over the chimney pots, carried on its arches, these suburban trains of the old London, Chatham and Dover Railway system run. You can look down from them into small back gardens. Spires of the south-London skyline rise out of trees. New building estates rise into the sky higher than the spires, and arid and sad they are. Here and there an elementary school, as it used to be called, in Queen Anne red brick and terra cotta, stands walled and sedate among Victorian dwellings.

But chiefly we think of these platforms 1 to 8 as the Gateway to the Continent and the Gateway from the Continent. The various para-phernalia of the Customs people at one end. The many offices there have to be in connection with foreign travel, the many different sorts of uniformed officials, all give a certain glamour to the Continental side of the station. Chief among these are the Wagon-Lits attendants on the Night-Ferry still used by the Duke of Windsor and Yehudi Menuhin and others who prefer rail and boat to air. You see the passengers with hopeful faces longing for wine and sunshine arriving much too early for the Continental trains and finding not half enough waiting rooms. Outside platform 8 you see parents anxiously awaiting the return of children from their holiday abroad, or you see a fussed English housewife waiting for an *au-pair* girl, and unable to find who she is, or whether she has really arrived. Some of the officials on the platform speak French. And here for the first time many a foreigner sees England. After that journey through the orchards of the garden of England, as Kent is called, what on earth do they think when they find the haphazard muddle of Victoria Station? Perhaps they think this is England. Certainly it is homely. It is only ostentatious when you look very carefully at the outside.

The lure of the Continent.

Left Victorian solidity and fragility on the Grosvenor Hotel.

BY STEAM from Paddington to New York, via Bristol, was the mighty dream of 27-year-old Isambard Kingdom Brunel when, in 1833, he was appointed civil engineer for the Great Western Railway project. The task was triumphantly completed within eight years – in about half the time it takes these days to build a motorway from London to Bristol. Bridges, viaduct, stations, Brunel took them in his stride and, with his mechanical engineer Daniel Gooch, constructed the great rail works in Swindon as the heart of the venture.

Not content with all this he had already launched his timber paddle-steamer, the Great Western, which reached New York in 1838, taking fifteen days for the trip. He followed it up with the Great Britain, an iron liner, which made New York in 1845. Some ten years later he produced the Great Eastern, 693 feet long and, at the time, five times bigger than any other ship in the world. It made the crossing in eleven days and caused Walt Whitman to burst into wonderment and verse.

Such was the genius of I. K. Brunel, born at Portsmouth, the cigar chain-smoking son of a French engineer who was employed from 1824 to 1842 in London constructing a tunnel under the Thames.

Meanwhile, the line from London to Bristol was extended to Plymouth, Penzance, Cardiff and Fishguard, to the Western Midlands and up to Birkenhead. The undergraduates of Oxford used Paddington; and so did Public Schools at Eton, Radley, Marlborough, Shrewsbury, Malvern and the now extinct Weymouth

Approaching the eleventh hour, Paddington time, on Number One platform.

College; hunting people got out at Badminton; carpet manufacturers at Kidderminster; coal owners at Cardiff; jewellers at Birmingham; valetudinarians at Torquay, Leamington, Cheltenham, Tenbury Wells and Tenby; sailors at Plymouth, Devonport and Falmouth; organists used it for the Three Choirs Festival at Worcester, Hereford or Gloucester. The Welsh who seem so often to be in trains, use it all the time.

Brunel still dominates Paddington station; it is admirably planned and copes with traffic greater than even he could have envisaged. It is the only London terminus with no exterior. When the line first started from London in 1838 the terminus in the stucco Grecian and leafy village of Paddington was a series of Soaneian arches. An artist and architect as well as an engineer, Brunel was excited about the new terminus to be built farther west of the old one. It was to be aisled cathedral in a cutting. Departing passengers came down a slope on the south side of the cutting. Arrivals left up a slope on the north side. They still do so today. The cutting is roofed over. Pillars of cast iron support a triple roof of wrought iron and glass. The central aisle is a hundred and two feet across and the side aisles are seventy and sixty-eight feet across. A fourth aisle was added to the north side in 1916.

Brunel was usually his own architect and built his country stations in styles that he thought suited their neighbourhood and he used local materials. The head office at Bristol and the original station and that at Bath were Tudor. Chippenham, Swindon and Reading were Italianate. Italianate was chosen for the entrance to Paddington which is at the south side of the cutting. But when he came into the station Brunel decided to call in an architect friend, Matthew Digby Wyatt, who designed iron work in the roof, capitals for the cast iron columns and the charming little bow-windowed affairs still on the first floor of Platform 1. These are in a style of Digby Wyatt's own invention nearer Elizabethan than anything. Owen Jones who designed the colour scheme for the Crystal Palace in 1851 designed the original colour scheme for Paddington, which was completed by 1854.

At the London end of the platforms was a garden at the back of the hotel which was

Opposite Great Western Board Room with its bow windows.

Above Symmetry in imminent departures for the west country.

known as the Lawn. The present concourse when one comes up from the Underground of the uncomfortable, slow, unreliable Inner Circle Railway or the infrequent Bakerloo Tube is still known as 'The Lawn' locally. To station announcers it is 'the main circulating area'.

The Great Western Hotel, opened in 1854, was not part of the Brunel scheme. It was built from the design of P. C. Hardwick who had helped his father design the mighty Roman Great Hall at Euston (now destroyed) and who designed the present Gothic Charterhouse School at Godalming. It was the first of the great railway hotels of London and in a baroque style suited to merchants whose eyes were looking beyond the English channel to the continent for trade. Its most splendid room was the dining room on the ground floor with caryatids supporting coved, baroque ceiling. This sumptuous interior and the rest of the hotel were redecorated in a most expensive pseudo-simple modernistic style in the 1930s from which the interior of the hotel has never recovered.

The station inside, whether you approach it lengthwise or sideways on, is still spacious, practical and satisfying. Something approaching the original colours of Owen Jones have been restored and they are much pleasanter than the dirty cream which Brunel's great greenhouse used to be.

When some of the other railways of England were amalgamated in the 1920s, the Great Western still stood out with its own name, its own green livery for the engines, brown and cream for carriages and stations, radishes and watercress in the dining cars and its own most excellent blend of whisky in the buffets. Its men were proud to be Great Western. To this day it is a west-country railway and Paddington is just the London end of a line that was born in Bristol, and whose remaining more reliable trains are those between Bristol and London. Before the advent of nationalisation and the gradual breaking of its spirit the Great Western was the best railway in the world.

GREAT CENTRAL RAILWAY! It was a grand name for a mighty line; people who said Manchester, Sheffield and Lincolnshire stood for Money Sunk and Lost said that G. C. meant Gone Completely. The first train steamed into the new terminus at Marylebone in March 1899. That prose poet of the railways, C. Hamilton Ellis, has a splendid description of the line in his book *The Trains We Loved*.

> The first Great Central London expresses showed a higher percentage of corridor stock than those of any other railway; they were lightly loaded and smartly timed; internally they were the most comfortable, while they perpetuated the old Sheffield Company's partiality for gorgeous decoration; Jason fought for the Golden Fleece in mezzotint panels on the dining car ceilings, and as you lounged on a splendiferous pew of carved oak and figured plush, the sun, shining through coloured glass deck lights, gave a deliciously bizarre quality to the complexion of the lady opposite. There were buffet cars long before any other company dared to introduce them.

I can remember the handsome 4-6-2 tank engines, and those acres of goods trucks with G. C. on them in the wide yards north of the terminus, and the Atlantic Class engines which pulled the few expresses. Sir Sam Fay, the famous General Manager from 1902 until 1922, was the first person to whom I wrote a fan letter. He was good enough to reply and I carried his letter on headed Great Central Railway stationery in my pocket for a whole school term.

I much envied my cousins who lived in Nottingham, for they could, had they wanted to do so, not only have arrived in the calm of Marylebone, but have crossed, sheltered by the still-existing iron marquee in front of the station, over the road to the Hotel Great Central itself. They would have stood dazed by its marble entrance hall, the wide stone staircase, and the painted tympana of nymphs and goddesses. They would have heard a string band in the distance, and following their ears would have found the glass-covered courtyard where it played and where palm trees shaded tables for tea. And in the evening maybe there would have been a trade banquet in the Wharncliffe Rooms which were Marylebone's answer to Liverpool Street's Abercorn Rooms. This great dining hall, as well as the public reception rooms, was all pure Maples-mahogany, marble, armorial stained glass, vast electroliers shining down on thick carpets and heavy cutlery from Sheffield. The architect of the Hotel Great Central was Colonel R. W. Edis, who designed part of the Great Eastern Hotel. At the hotel, the Colonel spared no expense on the exterior which is of golden terra cotta and with a central tower on the Marylebone Road front. The style seems to be Flemish Renaissance. There are many balconies and viewpoints in its elaborate façades for watching carriage traffic, buses and drays. Even today this refreshingly vulgar purse-proud building makes all the newer slabs erected near it since the war look cheap.

We just had enough money to run a little egg and dart motif along the terra cotta capitals.

Above Note the initials GCR in the railing.

Above right Private road between station and the Old Great Central Hotel.

Sir Blundell Maple, the merchant and race horse owner, financed the hotel. The Great Central had run out of cash by the time it reached the metropolis. The little terminus, three storeyed and of red brick, was not the work of a well known architect but the company's civil engineer. On the street side it looks like a branch public library in a Manchester suburb, it is durable and well built, and to this day the initials GCR can be seen in the railings. The refreshment rooms and waiting rooms have alas been done up 1950s 'contemporary', but one bar survives with its panelling and brackets and rich mahogany fitting in the old Great Central style. The station was never completed, so poor had the Great Central become. There are only three platforms, the other three were never used. Expensive and excellent tunnels were built under the Hampstead hills and under Lord's Cricket Ground. They too cannot all have been used, and no doubt today rat-ridden, dank and dripping,

there are tunnels waiting for the Great Central to duplicate its main line. But even that main line has disappeared and so have the excellent trains which once left Rugby (Central), Nottingham and Sheffield (Victoria) for Marylebone.

This was the last main line to London, and British Railways have taken their revenge on it for being so new and comfortable. It is still the best station for the thousands who live in Gerrard's Cross and Beaconsfield. There are always rumours that it will be shut down altogether. As for the Hotel Great Central it has been boringly renamed '222 Marylebone Road', and is the headquarters of British Railways. Needless to say the interior has so far as possible been gutted and done up with old-fashioned with-itry, where there were any architectural features, and left looking like a wartime government department everywhere else.

Colonel Edis's facade from which to watch carriages come down the Marylebone Road. All this in terra cotta too.

Old Euston Propylaeum by Hardwick, demolished in 1961 after the failure of a strong campaign for its preservation.

station architecture, the persistent idea in the 1830s was that the railway station 'was to the modern city what the city gate was to the ancient city'. Therefore a mighty undertaking like the London and Birmingham must be symbolised by a monumental entrance. An architect Philip Hardwick (1792–1870), a Royal Academician, and himself the son of a classic architect of talent and versatility, was summoned to produce a gateway from England's capital and heart, London, to her stomach and toyshop, Birmingham. The portico was best seen in its original state, especially at an oblique angle. Alas! no one living can remember the completed design, though a beautiful water-colour and numerous prints remind us of it. The central feature was a Doric portico or Propylaeum, simple and huge. Between the fluted columns, each eight-and-a-half feet in diameter, which formed the main carriage entrance, might be glimpsed the green hills of Hampstead beyond. Either side of the portico were pairs of square stone lodges, adorned with flat pilasters. Each lodge had a grand Doric central door, and the whole composition was joined together by a cast-iron screen of gates, lofty and ornamental, by J. J. Bramah, the locksmith and inventor. The grand entrance was never intended to be more than a monument to railway achievement, as was the terminus at Curzon Street, Birmingham, which has an Ionic portico by the same architect.

When they were completed, the columns of the Euston Propylaeum, built of stone (from Bramley quarries, Yorkshire) by W. and L. Cubitt, were higher than those of any other building in London at the time.

There seem to be in many an architect streaks of puritan and prig. Hardwick's introduction from Euston to the Midlands soon came in for criticism. It was purely ornamental. It served no purpose. It showed up the unworthiness of the humble train sheds for Stephenson's railway behind it. Pugin made it the subject of one of his funniest caricatures. It wasn't Gothic, it wasn't even Roman. It was old-fashioned.

There is no doubt that the comfort of passengers needed more attention. There were often long waits at the terminus. The portico was insufficient protection and the train sheds

THE LONDON and Birmingham was the first trunk railway in the world and it was in operation by 1837. Though the Stockton and Darlington, Liverpool and Manchester, London and Greenwich and many lesser lines were earlier, the London and Birmingham was the greatest railway event of its kind. As Carroll Meeks points out in his interesting and informative history of railway

were draughty. In 1846 Philip Hardwick with the aid of his son, Philip C. Hardwick (1822–1892) designed the Great Hall at Euston. Many will remember this. It was one of London's finest public rooms. Here the passengers could wait in palatial splendour until officials came in and rung a bell and announced the time of departure of trains. Passengers waited on the ground floor. They could ascend by a double staircase and watch the crowds below from a gallery which surrounded the whole enormous hall. The style of the hall was Roman Ionic and it was lit by attic windows which cast strong shadow on the elaborately corbelled and coffered ceiling. A statue of George Stephenson dominated the hall and the double staircase. The double staircase led to the Shareholders' Meeting Room which was of a sumptuous and Baroque elegance never equalled in English railway architecture. The survival of the Great Hall and Meeting Room from German bombing made up for the sad incursions by railway architects in the late nineteenth and early twentieth centuries into the original Hardwick Propylaeum. The outer lodges were soon demolished; the remaining pair, which served to give scale to the huge Doric columns and antae, were defaced by notices and hoardings. They survived until 1967. Despite protests from preservation societies, the London County Council and even the Royal Fine Art Commission, nothing could stop the architects of British Railways from destroying every vestige of old Euston. The demolition contractor, Mr Valori, so much disliked destroying the portico, that he offered to number its stones and re-erect them at his own expense on a site chosen by British Railways. The architects refused this offer and Mr Valori presented to the newly-formed Victorian Society a silver model of the propylaeum which the late Lord Esher, then the Society's chairman, received with a witty and sadly ironic speech made at the expense of the barbarians who ran British Railways.

What masterpiece arose on the site of the old station? No masterpiece. Instead there is a place where nobody can sit; an underground taxi-entrance so full of fumes that drivers, passengers and porters alike hate it. A great hall of glass looks like a mini-version of London Airport, which it seems to be trying to imitate. On its expanse of floor and against its walls passengers lie and await trains, which they are not allowed to enter from the platforms below without the permission of uniformed gendarmes at the barriers, who imprison the travellers in the hall until the last possible moment. A constant stream of lengthy official verbiage pours over the waiting queues: 'buffet car and refreshment facilities will be available on this service', 'will Mr MacAlpine awaiting a passenger from Crewe kindly contact the Information desk'; hygienic and slippery buffets may be glimpsed on upper floors, and less hygienic and more slippery bars are entered from the hall itself. The telephone boxes are open to the full blast of the Tannoy system and the Irish drunks who have always haunted Euston. You can see people with their hands to one ear and the receiver to the other, trying to make themselves understood. The smell of sweat and used clothes, even in winter, is strong in this hall, for there is something funny about the air conditioning. In hot weather it is cooler to go to the empty space in front of the station, where the portico could easily have been rebuilt. In cold weather it is advisable to retreat into one of the shops. The only place where the air approaches freshness and reasonable temperature is down several flights to the Underground station, with its manifold passages.

A passenger who had a weak heart, arriving in London at Euston, had better go home again without attempting the long upward slope from the platform, where the trains arrive, to the hall. After that there will be the long walk across the hall and an almost equally long walk to the fume-ridden taxi-rank with its queues. Alternatively there are the complications of the Underground station.

I have heard the excuse made for this disastrous and inhuman structure, which seems to ignore passengers, that British Railways originally intended to make it pay by adding multi-storey hotels and office blocks to the flat roof. This seems a lame excuse for so inhospitable a building.

It was opened by the Queen in 1968.

THIRTY YEARS LATER

Alan A. Jackson

IN CONTRAST to the quarter century following the Second World War, the years 1972–2002 saw much interesting and radical alteration and rebuilding at most of London's termini. Following the ruthless purge of everything historic at Euston and the inadequacies of its replacement, so roundly criticised in the final chapter of Sir John Betjeman's book, the vigilance, activity and influence of the conservationists was greatly increased. They attained an early minor victory at St Pancras and a major one at Liverpool Street, the latter much eased when the decision to close the Broad Street terminus enabled most of the lucrative office developments to be located outside Liverpool Street station's footprint.

Elsewhere, sacrifice of the historic high train sheds and other Victorian infrastructure was less easy to control in the fierce drive to obtain maximum profit from station redevelopment by selling the air space above the platforms. Even at Liverpool Street, the East Side was built over whilst at Charing Cross, Cannon Street, Fenchurch Street and the Central side of Victoria all the platforms were enclosed in basement-like spaces beneath the low ceilings formed by the rafts supporting multi-tiered superstructure. Beyond, in desperate pursuit of maximum returns to railway funds, the concourses and other spaces were flooded with retail units and eating and drinking places of various kinds. The grandeur that had once been a feature of arriving and departing from these London termini was replaced by an impression that one had fallen asleep and upon waking found the train coming to a stop at what seemed to be a tunnel platform; and, after alighting, the walk to the taxi, bus or Underground was suggestive of passing through a shopping mall. Protests were voiced but no other practical alternatives were on offer to finance the much needed modernisation of these important stations.

Until the early 1970s, BR's attitude towards its Victorian and Edwardian heritage had been one of indifference, even hostility, but this gradually changed to become more sensitive and sympathetic, particularly under the 1976–83 chairmanship of Sir Peter Parker. The pressure for office development was further increased by the 1986 deregulation of the Stock Exchange (the 'Big Bang'), when the City of London Corporation, anxious to prevent firms moving out to the cheaper redeveloped Docklands sites, readily granted planning permission for new building on railway land around its boundaries. The Liverpool Street/Broadgate scheme was particularly well-sited and happily-timed to reap maximum benefits from this situation. Through most of the 1980s British Rail was able to promote joint development schemes which would rake in useful profits for the railway, notably in London at Fenchurch Street, Cannon Street, Charing Cross, Liverpool Street and Victoria.

Three termini find no place in the survey that follows. Broad Street disappeared in the rebuilding of Liverpool Street, replaced by a connection at Graham Road, Hackney designed to allow trains to run between north west London and Liverpool Street, a service which lasted only till September 1992, but much of the Broad Street–Dalston alignment is now being refurbished for extension of the London Underground East London Line. Holborn Viaduct was completely demolished after its last public train left on 26 January 1990, to be replaced at a lower level by City Thameslink, a new through station whose long platforms could be accessed from both Ludgate Hill and Holborn Viaduct. Finally, the Euston of today is not included here since it had already been totally rebuilt in time for Sir John to record his reactions in his book. It has not been substantially altered since.

We now look in some detail at the developments and changes of the past thirty years at each of those stations which still retain elements of their original construction.

1

3

2

ST PANCRAS

The miserable death of Old Euston proved to be something of a turning point, strengthening the influence and resolve of the guardians of our architectural heritage. Thus when in 1978 British Rail rashly proposed a new ticket office and travel centre at St Pancras in anodised aluminium and matt brown melamine plastic, made visible from the concourse by alterations in the four gothic-arched openings on that side,

Camden Council, spurred on by the Victorian Society and other defenders of the faith, refused planning permission.

When the refurbished booking hall opened in May 1983 it was seen to be a sympathetic restoration; the linenfold panelled oak ticket office was retained, moved from the east wall to the west side with a new floor laid around it (1).

Inside the train shed, alterations could be less sensitive and

4

5

compromises were possible. In 1982 the platform barrier line was modernised and given an electronic train departure indicator, at the cost of some damage to the scale of the concourse.

After closure in June 1972 of the adjoining Somers Town freight depot, the 11-acre site was used for the new British Library building opened in 1997.

When the 1868 train shed roof was extensively repaired in 1980 opportunity was taken to remove the 18ft diameter Victorian clock mounted on the south screen. This had ceased to function in the 1960s and had latterly lost its 7ft and 4ft 6in hands. During its removal, the dial was damaged but the clock was purchased as scrap by Roland Hoggard, a passenger train guard whose hobby was collecting railway clocks. He removed it piece by piece in his guard's van and then to his farm barn in the Nottingham village of Thurgarton, where he managed to get it into working order. During 1985, with Mr Hoggard's help, BR made plastic moulds from the original clock and using these, had by early 1986 built and installed in its old position an electrically-worked replica with a glass fibre face (2). This provided a fine finishing touch to the thorough cleaning of the station interior (3) completed in 1983, an operation which had included the fitting of roof floodlights to provide near-daylight levels of

6

7

8

artificial illumination. The train shed lighting was further improved in 1994–95.

Outside, the removal of decades of soot and encrusted grime from Scott's frontages had been started in 1977 with the aid of funds from central government and the Greater London Council. Alas, the cost and extent of this task was underestimated, leading to its being left uncompleted when the money ran out in 1981. Twelve years then passed before cleaning was resumed. The butterfly emerged from its chrysalis in October 1994, when all who had known this building through its many years in a drab black coat were surprised by the eye-catching display of rose-tinted bricks (4–8).

The problem of what to do with the empty hotel dragged on unsolved for many years. After railway staff had vacated it in 1984 Camden Council, potential developers and BR

9

became enmeshed in interminable arguments which were eventually overtaken by an economic recession that served to check lavish proposals to modernise the interior. Meanwhile rainwater continued to penetrate the leaky roof, rotting the woodwork beneath.

Not before time, the roof was totally renewed and water damage repaired in a £10m 1994–95 overhaul initiated by the BR chairman, Sir Bob Reid. This project included

careful cleaning of the internal mural decoration, including that in the vaulted ceiling of the main staircase (9). During 1996 ownership was transferred to London & Continental Railways, a company charged with developing St Pancras as London's main terminal for Channel Tunnel rail traffic. It was then arranged that the main part of the building would be modernised internally to become a 21st century luxury hotel, the Marriott St Pancras, its top three

floors to be remodelled as residential apartments.

The Barlow train shed and George Gilbert Scott's Gothic frontage were to remain in place but the interior of the station was to be completely rearranged and rebuilt on a new concrete deck, its platforms extended to 400 metres to accommodate the long Eurostar trains. The outer, or northern end would have 13 platforms, the extra ones allocated to the present Midland train services and the new

domestic Kent services. The extended and new platforms were to be enclosed in a steel and aluminium and glass box, wider than the original roof on the east side, its 21st century design contrasting boldly with the Victorian architecture and engineering immediately to its south. At its south end, the top of the new roof would be level with the springing line of the arch of Barlow's train shed, its design allowing entry of plenty of natural light.

10

11

KINGS CROSS

Two major problems at Kings Cross were remedied in the 1970s. The cumulative muddle of the approach tracks was disentangled after a good deal of taxing work carried through in the midst of normal traffic. From 3 April 1977 the layout as far as Finsbury Park was rearranged in a simplified, more rational way. Rebuilding the former freight flyover north of the Copenhagen Tunnels allowed Up suburban trains to be brought into the west side of the terminus, eliminating most of the conflicting movements between these and main line services.

Platforms at Kings Cross were renumbered 1–14 east to west from 1 May 1972 but with the track rearrangements completed in 1977 and diversion of many suburban trains south of Finsbury Park via Drayton Park to Moorgate in 1976 two of the former seven suburban platforms were deemed sufficient for the remaining services. Numbers 11–13 were therefore shut from December 1976 and 11 was later filled in to widen 10. From 5 March 1977 platform 14 and York Road, the Up suburban platform on the east side of the station, were also closed. As almost always, electrification built up traffic and by the end of the 1980s, more platform space was needed. To meet this requirement, platform 11 was restored from 3 October 1988.

Around the same time, the suburban station received the Network SouthEast treatment with a revamped concourse, plants, a new ticket barrier, retail units and terrazzo floor tiling.

Lack of funds and also perhaps a new and more cautious attitude towards disturbing historic fabric led to the second problem at Kings Cross, its cramped concourse and inadequate ticket offices, being tackled less thoroughly than the rationalisation of the

12

13

track layout. After clearing the jumble of buildings in the forecourt area up to Euston Road, the site was covered with a 16,000 sq ft single-storey structure providing concourse space, shops and a travel centre with a 110ft counter dispensing tickets, reservations and information. Opened on 3 June 1973, this allowed covered access to the Underground ticket hall and a new taxi rank on the west side. Although an improvement to the previous situation, the

1973 accretion was unworthy of the Victorian frontage it partially obscured. It was very much a temporary solution and showed it; some features wore quickly and refurbishment was mounted after only ten years. By the opening of the new century it had outlived its time-limited planning consent by eight years.

In 1995–98 Lewis Cubitt's 1852 frontage was again cleaned and restored, the work including refurbishment

of John Edward Dent's fine triple-dial turret clock, whose chimes had been silent since 1924. This restoration, assisted by a grant from the Railway Heritage Trust, included electric operation of the clock and installation of tape-recorded chimes of the hours and quarters amplified by loudspeakers (11).

Inside the train shed, changes since 1972 have been confined to the superficial and cosmetic (12). In 1995 the large

drum clock on the footbridge above platforms 7 and 8 was restored, again with the help of the Railway Heritage Trust (10). An English Heritage blue plaque in memory of the London & North Eastern Railway's steam locomotive engineer Sir Nigel Gresley was unveiled outside the western entrance in September 1997 (13).

14

15

LIVERPOOL STREET

This station's location at the edge of the City made it possible for British Rail to contemplate rebuilding strategies which could be financed from commercial development of the air space above the platforms, a bonus arising after conversion to electric traction. It subsequently became clear that it might be possible to close the relatively little-used Broad Street terminus and its approach tracks to release further land for office blocks. The first detailed scheme emerged in 1975, proposing a concrete station with 22 platforms, a hotel, shops and passenger amenities, this to be surrounded by and buried under office buildings on what the Victorian Society described as an 'overpowering scale'. A Liverpool Street Station Campaign was soon busy, co-ordinating and driving the powerful opposition from the heritage bodies. Although BR then came forward with a revised scheme offering minimal non-railway development over the station, it still proposed to remove most of the existing structures.

With the enthusiastic opposition of the Campaign and well-researched evidence of the historic and archi-tectural importance of the terminus and its curtilage presented by the Greater London Council's Historic Buildings Division, the outline planning enquiry proved a difficult one for the promoters.

Eventually permission to go ahead was granted only on condition that the 1875 West Side train shed (described by the campaigners as 'a cast iron cathedral of the railway age') would be kept, along with C E Barry's 1884 Great Eastern Hotel and R W Edis's Abercorn Rooms. Working with developers, BR then produced further plans which envisaged extensive areas of new office space in a group of five buildings comprising 'Broadgate' on the site of Broad Street station and over the adjacent approach tracks of both stations and 'Bishops-gate', to be erected above platforms 11–18.

Like the earlier proposals, these incorporated a substantial amount of retail, restaurant and café space; 'Broadgate' was to be linked to the new station concourse by a shopping mall which would form a third main entrance to Liverpool Street station. Legislation for the project was secured by BR and London Transport in 1983 but another two years elapsed before private funding was arranged. A start was then made in partnership with Rosehaugh Stanhope Developments plc on demolition of the unwanted railway structures and the new construction, a task which was to take almost six years, during which BR doggedly and successfully continued to keep its train services running.

16

17

March 1988 saw the first part of the new station finished – the 'superloos' below the new concourse. Still incomplete in several respects, the new Liverpool Street was declared open by H M Queen Elizabeth II on 5 December 1991.

Its architects and engineers had weaved a brilliantly successful blend of the best of the original Victorian elements with accurate replicas of features of the old station (*14*) and pastiche 'neo-Victorian' innovations such as the twin towers at the main entrances in Liverpool Street (*15*) and Bishopsgate, these inspired by a corner tower of the retained Great Eastern Hotel. There were also some uncompromisingly modern components, notably the upper walkways and bridges, the two-level white steel and glass trading units (*17*, *21*) and the larger but similar glazed vaulting over the escalators at the Bishopsgate entrance. Offering a lively and strong contrast with the rest, these were designed not to obstruct enjoyment of the vistas within the interior.

Here indeed was Old Euston's revenge, demonstrating how it was possible for the fine work of 19th-century engineers and architects to be respected and felicitously blended with late 20th-century architecture and station design. Indeed, looking up to the roof,

many would find it difficult to determine which was new and which was the original 1875 ironwork made resplendent with a restored tracery of cut-out patterns in its spandrels and leafy capitals on its columns (*16*, *17*, *20*).

In the process of remodelling, much of the old station was demolished. Of the railway office buildings around the southern and eastern curtilage, the northern parts of 50 Liverpool Street were razed but the south pavilion was rebuilt with a ground floor arcade forming the east side of the main entrance piazza (*18*). The war-damaged Hamilton House and its near neighbour Harwich House, both in Bishopsgate, were knocked down.

A great deal more disappeared, including the 1894 East Side train shed and the delightful jettied gazebo tea rooms on the East and West Sides.

The new station offered a broad level concourse running straight along the heads of all its 18 platforms, linked to Liverpool Street and Bishopsgate by escalators, stairs and lifts (*23*). This central feature remedied a major design defect of its predecessor, transforming Betjeman's 'dark cathedral' into a veritable palace of light. Most of the platforms were extended and given calling-on facilities to allow two trains to occupy them simultaneously.

20

18

19

Pedestrian and road movements were carefully segregated with the taxi access road moved over to the far west side at concourse level. Above it was a bus station, its vehicles visible to those coming from arriving trains.

A wide entrance to the Underground ticket hall, also located at the west end of the concourse, exhibited one of the rare blemishes in the new design. The transition between the two spaces was by a flight of ten steps, presenting an awkward hazard for the elderly and infirm and all encumbered with luggage.

To strengthen the link between the new and what had gone before, BR architect Nick Derbyshire decorated the remodelled station with many reminders and resited relics of the old Great Eastern Railway terminus. A railing decoration representing the GER coat of arms was beautifully restored (19). Exact replicas were made of some old features such as the Portland stone piers now placed around the piazzas at the main entrances (14, 18).

Alongside the north wall of the Great Eastern Hotel the archway of the old cab road remained, decorated with re-used

21

22

23

carved spandrel panels (*23*). Carved brick lunettes were saved and re-positioned, as were the War Memorial (from the old ticket hall) and decorative lettering (from Harwich House) placed above it (*22*). We leave readers to discover other examples of what Nick Derbyshire described as 'enrichment' if they find themselves at Liverpool Street with a little time to spare.

With the final phases of the Broadgate Extension recently completed above the approach tracks between Worship and Primrose Streets, the Liverpool Street and Broad Street railway lands development, providing over four million square feet of office space over and around a remodelled railway terminus represents one of the largest rebuilding projects ever carried out in the City of London in modern times. For BR it was a financial success, generating enough to leave a substantial surplus after funding all the railway works, including the Integrated Electronic Control Centre (IECC) opened on 2 April 1989.

FENCHURCH STREET

By allowing office developers to make use of its air space, BR mustered enough money for a total rebuilding of the interior of Fenchurch Street between 1984 and 1990. Of the station John Betjeman knew, this left only the listed 1853 Railway Place frontage, sketched out by (Sir) William Tite and adapted by the engineer George Berkeley.

Work on construction of 'Fenchurch Exchange', 92,000 sq ft of offices over the inner ends of the platforms, started late in 1983. This involved removal of the Berkeley train shed roof, although its outline survives as the curve at the top of the frontage. Payments to BR funded a thorough restoration of the 1853 elevations (24) and a major refurbishment of this busy station, which by this time was being used by around 65,000 passengers every weekday, 17,000 more than Paddington. Improvements completed by September 1987 included enlargement of the concourse by setting back the barrier line and centrally-sited escalators to carry passengers to and from street level at the west end of the station. This last involved the removal of the two staircases with cast iron balustrades mentioned and shown on page 49 as well as replacement of the old wooden booking office opposite the Railway Place entrance.

A second, much more extensive building, sited mostly over the eastern end of the station, was begun two years later. 'Number One America Square', 200ft high, containing some 209,000 sq ft of air-conditioned office space, was bounded by Coopers Row, Crosswall, America Square and railway land to the south. Completed early in 1991, much of its space was initially taken by Baring's Bank. BR's purse received enough to finance further modernisation, including longer platforms with new awnings, updated lighting and terrazzo decor. A welcome improvement in this phase was the replacement of the dingy and shabby Crosswall entrance and ticket office with a ticket hall in the railway arches on the east side of Coopers Row. Opened in April 1990, this gave those using the Underground improved access to Tower Hill station.

25

LONDON BRIDGE

London Bridge stood high in the list of termini requiring rearrangement and rebuilding. Financed partly by property deals and partly by central government funds, the work, designed by BR architect N.D.T. Wikely was not finished until the end of 1979 and had to be undertaken with minimal interference to the station's intensive train services.

Around the outer or north eastern curve of Station Approach the remains of the war-damaged LB&SCR and SER buildings were demolished in 1970, after

which a wide concourse was formed for both the through and terminal platforms with ticket office, travel centre, parcels block, retail units and a buffet bar. The bus station was resited under an extension of the new concourse roofing. Order and unity were imparted after many years of muddle, with all platforms linked by a wide covered footbridge across the whole station, opened in December 1974. Although the old LB&SCR train shed was re-roofed in 1973–74, the general form and appearance of this part of the station (25) was not greatly

altered apart from the insertion of the new footbridge.

In the early 1970s the 1966–67 Oldham Estate tower in the forecourt received a companion in the form of a 230,000 sq ft office building erected by Peachey Properties on the south west side of the former LB&SCR terminus which was leased to Price Waterhouse. This helped to subsidise some of the works already described.

The approach tracks were rebuilt in 1972–78 to minimise conflicting movements, maximise capacity and allow reversible working. From

20 April 1976 a large new signal box controlled 47 route miles extending from Charing Cross and Cannon Street over much of the south east suburban area.

London Bridge station now faces further rearrangement and rebuilding as it is adapted to play its role in the Thameslink 2000 project. This much-delayed proposal is designed to increase the capacity and variety of Thameslink services, giving London at least one through main line rail system which will stand some comparison with the *Réseau Express Régional* in Paris.

CANNON STREET

Only the partial skeleton of John Hawkshaw's 1866 Cannon Street station remains today.

The foreshortened flank walls (26) and twin 130ft riverside towers now look as smart as the day they were finished, standing proudly and boldly out from a nest of modern horizontal and vertical architecture (27).

The mid 1960s had seen the completion of the J.G.L. Poulson curtain-walled office blocks at the northern end of the station: a 17-storey frontage building, a lower one over the northern ends of the platforms and a third in Bush Lane alongside, but the associated BR remodelling continued into the early 1970s. After demolition of the old shops along the forecourt frontage, the Underground ticket hall and platforms were rebuilt and new girderwork placed over the District line tracks to allow widening of the roadway. A new street level concourse, reached by stairs from the platforms, was formed above the London Transport ticket hall. With its ticket office, travel centre and six retail units, this was finally ready for use in March 1974, a date which marked the completion of the first phase of modernisation. Above, much of the platforms were open to the sky between the gaunt Victorian side walls which had supported the

long-dismantled arch of the train shed, the only shelter from wind and weather given by crude steel and corrugated asbestos cement canopies erected in the late 1960s.

With two thirds of the cost covered by a grant from The Railway Heritage Trust, the smoke-blackened 1866 walls and towers were scrubbed clean in 1986. This improvement presaged the building of 289,000 sq ft of offices in six storeys on a steel deck over the platforms at the southern end. Completed

in 1991, this structure, vaguely reminiscent of the prow of an ocean liner, was supported by columns that ran through the vaults below the station to stand on 450 bored pile foundations. The higher rear section was given its splayed elevation to preserve views of St Paul's Cathedral. To mark the long-delayed completion of the rebuilt terminus, BR refurbished and improved the concourse, adding new shops and entrance, completing the work in July 1990.

26

27

28

29

BLACKFRIARS

This station was the only one whose reconstruction BR financed from its own purse. Richard Seifert & Partners designed the new building, which included an entrance hall shared with London Transport and an expanded high level concourse with ticket office, reached by escalator from street level. Beyond, all the old wooden platforms and the roofing over them were reconstructed (28). Someone saved the 54 stone frontage blocks bearing the names of near and far distant places originally served by the London, Chatham & Dover Railway from this station. These were brought up and placed against the west wall of the new concourse. The BR part of the project was completed in 1977.

The western and older river bridge, which had been used since 1864 by trains running to Ludgate Hill and Holborn Viaduct and through to the City Widened Lines at Farringdon, carried its last train in March 1969. It was removed early in 1985 by the floating crane that had raised the Mary Rose from the bed of the Solent in 1982. The large iron LC&DR coat of arms on its northern abutment was preserved, splendidly repainted (29).

A new bridge over Queen Victoria Street was completed at the end of 1974, and since 1990 has been used by cross-London Thameslink services.

WATERLOO

In the 1980s Waterloo was at the head of the passenger league but has since been overtaken by Victoria. Much remains that John Betjeman would recognise. He might even approve of some changes, such as the cleaned stonework which has brought Scott's architectural detail more clearly to the eye (*31, 32, 33, 34*); the 1995–96 restoration of the 1919 Synchronome four-face master-clock, complete with its original 24-hour markings (*35*) and the 1988 demolition of MacDonald's 1934 cinema.

Less pleasing for him would be the disappearance of the Surrey Room and the Windsor Tea Rooms (both closed in May 1973) although the latter's domed Edwardian pay kiosks remain in the 1977 Travel Centre which the Windsor became. The Long Bar, which JB mentions, made way for a combined main line and suburban 16-window ticket office in 1970–71 and the handsome and impressive main line ticket hall was converted to a self-service catering facility, rejigged in various forms from May 1973 onwards.

A new barrier line for all the platforms, with sales kiosks and staff accommodation and station control room above it at platforms 6–11 and 20–21, was ready in autumn 1977.

30

31

32

Away went the Edwardian Bostwick gates with their decorative iron-work and down came the wooden departure and arrival indicators. Solari displays took their place.

Waterloo's long, curving concourse, arguably the finest of all in London's termini, was rendered brighter and more cheerful by white terrazzo tiling in 1983 (*30*). Access to the Waterloo East through platforms on the Charing Cross-London Bridge line became easier after completion in 1993 of a covered high level walkway reached by two escalators and two stairways from the centre of the concourse, these pushing through the site of the old Surrey Room.

Enter Railtrack plc, in 1996 proud new owner at knock-down price of all BR's infrastructure, including Waterloo. Eager for profits for its new shareholders, it was soon at work elaborating and expanding the retail units in and around the concourse, including the lower floor of the former railway offices which had been vacated in 1992 and subsequently refurbished. There was also some expenditure on items closer to the building's purpose: a subsidiary ticket office on the site of the left luggage facility at the south-east end of the concourse in 2000 and a state of the art train information system in the following spring with a main display that many found difficult to read in strong daylight.

33

34

Outside the station, the Southern Railway's Modern-style 1936 signal box with its outdated equipment was manned for the last time on 30 October 1990. On 2 April 1991, after a period of operation from a temporary panel, all movements into and out of Waterloo were controlled by the new Waterloo Area Signalling Centre in the former Wimbledon West Yard. Some track changes in the Waterloo throat took place at this time.

Both these events were driven by an important and pleasing new feature about to be incorporated into this Edwardian terminus – a London term-inus for new Eurostar trains.

The magnificent and beautifully-fenestrated sister-station, the Channel Tunnel International Terminal, was given the site of the 1885 'Windsor Side' platforms, 16–21.

35

station approaches mentioned above, the BR section of Waterloo lost two platforms and one of its approach tracks, a sacrifice made more tolerable by the withdrawal of practically all parcels, mail and newspaper traffic in 1988 and the cessation of almost all locomotive working in the early 1990s.

Designed by Nicholas Grimshaw and built by Bovis, the splendid terminus for the Channel Tunnel services has five platforms, numbered 20–24. Beneath 23 and 24 at levels minus one and minus two is a spacious Arrivals Concourse aligned alongside the new road approach between the station and York Road. Immediately below 20–23 is the Departures Lounge, whilst catering facilities occupy much of the next level down and the basement beneath this is allocated to car parking.

The glory of the new terminus is its elegant 400-metre steel and glass train shed, gently snaking against the north western flank of the Edwardian terminus. Grimshaw and his assistant architects had composed a truly inspiring structure recalling the great Victorian train sheds but also modern in spirit and form, reflecting the lines of the handsome air-smoothed Eurostar trains it sheltered (36, 37). Its three-pin arch, with centre pin to one side, produced asymmetrical

Preparations began in 1990 with the construction of two new BR platforms on the site of the old cab road between 11 and 12, using this space to extend the former loading dock roads. Opened on 2 July 1990, these were numbered 12 and 13 and the former 1–15 became 1–17. The old Windsor station was closed in two stages, platforms 16–18 on 30 June 1990 and 19–21 the following December. 'The Village', two storeys of offices and shops dating from 1920, was then demolished and two further platforms, 18 and 19, of 12-car length, were extended over its site, coming into use on 4 October 1993. Inhabitants of 'The Village' were rehoused in a new structure over platforms 1–10.

With these changes and the 1990–91 track rearrangement in the

36

geometry which accommodated the required train clearances whilst meeting the constraints imposed by the raised viaduct foundations which left only a narrow strip each side in which to place the roof supports. Recreating the glamour of international rail travel, Grimshaw rightly and boldly advertised the station's purpose and activity by making its interior clearly visible both from the main Waterloo concourse and the approach road alongside (*36*). Writing in *The Daily Telegraph Magazine*, Deyan Sudjic enthusiastically greeted this fine building as 'the single most impressive piece of railway architecture that Britain has seen since the heyday of station building in the 19th century... one of London's, if not Europe's, great public spaces.'

In a station designed to handle 6,000 passengers an hour it was essential to segregate the arriving and departing flows. Those boarding trains had the choice of several approaches to the Departure Concourse set below that of the main station. Coming by taxi or car, they entered on the same level as the roadway; arriving by Underground, they had level access from that ticket hall; and coming from the main line station, they used escalators or lifts to carry them down to the lower level. From above, those bound for mainland Europe, their trains, and the lengthy departures indicator and clock over the entry gates provided constant interest for those in the main station with time to spare. After entry checks, the international passengers passed into the Departures Lounge to

await their call to the escalator or ramp which would take them up to the point on the platform nearest to their seat on the train. Passengers from mainland Europe descended by escalators from platform level to the space below the entry level area before going out into the Arrival Concourse at street level.

Waterloo International was finished precisely on time in May 1993 but delays in completing the Channel Tunnel postponed its opening for public train services until 14 November 1994.

From 1970 onwards the Underground stations beneath Waterloo were gradually extended and enhanced to meet increasing traffic. By the end of 1999 the original ticket hall had been enlarged, and with the opening of the Jubilee Line Extension station under Waterloo Road on 20 November 1999 there

were 23 escalators and three lifts. London Transport's glass-walled Jubilee Line ticket hall was built into the north west end of the colonnade along Waterloo Road and in 1999–2001 this feature was refurbished and given escalators to link Waterloo Road with the main concourse at its south-east end, these supplementing another pair, opened in June 1997, between the north-west end and a new bus lay-by in Tenison Way.

Amidst all this modernisation, the two Waterloo & City tube platforms were not overlooked; a complete makeover including new flooring and platform edges was finished in 1986.

Although retaining some signs of its opulent Edwardian elegance, Waterloo entered the 21st century well-equipped to face further traffic growth.

38

39

CHARING CROSS

Beyond its refurbished concourse and frontage, the platform area of this conveniently-sited terminus is now hidden by commercial exploitation of the air space. John Betjeman would however be grateful that the hotel (38) and the concourse clock (39) survive, the former let in 1985 on a long lease. It seems unlikely he would find anything kind to say about the rest.

Commercial development began with railway-owned land in Craven Street, where 'Strand Central', an office block with retail premises at street level was built alongside the south west end of the station forecourt. A joint development by the BRPB and John McLean Associates, this was completed in 1986 without controversy but it did require demolition of the rather pleasing two-storey pavilion erected in the forecourt in 1898 for Thomas Cook & Son.

A new roof completed in 1985 had a remarkably brief life. In 1987–91 the air space over the platforms was filled with 'Embankment Place' (40), 347,000 sq ft of office space, a development undertaken jointly by the BRPB and the Greycoat Group. Designed in Post-Modern style by Terry Farrell & Co., this barrel-shaped steel structure with concrete floors rose to nine storeys, its weight supported on piles driven 100ft into the clay below the station. With it came an extension of the Hungerford Bridge footway in an arcade above Villiers Street. Its construction included redevelopment of the

40

42

41

whole area below the platforms, including removal of the Victorian cobbled street which had enabled cabs to drive up into the station before departing with their fares through the arch at the south west end of the frontage.

Farrell's design was nothing if not bold and challenging. It offered two railway references: the river front was decorated with a new version of the SR lettering and badge (41) that in different styles dated back to 1906 when the lettering was 'SECR'; and its arched

profile, when viewed from the river and the South Bank (42), recalled the outer end of John Hawkshaw's ill-fated roof. As an architectural statement, this was not without an element of unconscious irony; in the interests of maximising development gain, railway passengers now had a low-ceilinged cavern, artificially-lit throughout the day, instead of a light and airy train shed.

Simultaneously with Embankment Place, BR refurbished and rearranged the concourse and barrier line, the latter

surmounted with staff accommodation, station manager's office and station control room. On the ground floor of the frontage were a new ticket office and a travel centre soon replaced by retail space. In the confined concourse, made more cheerful by terrazzo tiling and cleaned brickwork, a sizeable block of retail units further impeded passenger movement at peak periods. Outside, the replica Eleanor Cross and the boundary stonework were cleaned, the columns along the

Strand given replica Victorian lamp globes. All was finished by the end of 1989.

In summer 1990 the platform area received glitzy decor and lighting in the style of the Farrell building above but this did little to minimise the effect of the low ceiling and loss of natural light. In 1998 and early 1999 the 32,000 sq ft of the glazed concourse roof was completely refurbished and rebuilt to further increase the contrast between this area and that beyond the barrier line.

43

44

45

VICTORIA

Something had to be done about Victoria. Historically it was two stations, with the LC&DR (and for a time GWR) on the south east or 'Eastern' side (*44*) and the LB&SCR on the north west, 'Central' or 'Brighton' side (*45*). After the 1923 grouping, the SR had made holes in the dividing wall but otherwise left things much as before. Drastic and total rebuilding and rearrangement was needed but in response to commercial and traffic pressures, the alterations drifted slowly into a compromise between old and new, financed by selling the air space above the Central side. As elsewhere where this had been done, trains in that part of the station were destined to be confined

46   47

in an artificially-lit
low-ceilinged area as
characterless as a large
underground car park,
despite strong lighting
and bright colours. But,
as we shall see, there
were also some positive
factors.

A stainless steel ticket
office for the whole
station was opened on
the Central side in 1976
and the concourse south
of it was enlarged in 1979
by setting the barrier
lines further south.

During 1979–80 the
internal and external
stone and brick surfaces
in both stations were
thoroughly cleaned,
bringing to notice much
hitherto unregarded
Edwardian architectural
detail (*46, 47, 48*).

The first phase of office
and shop building over
the lengthy LB&SCR train
shed was completed at
the end of 1984. 'Victoria
Plaza', a six-storey block
offering 220,000 sq ft of
office space, was jointly
developed by the BR
Property Board and
Greycoat London Estates
Group.

Designed by Elsom,
Pack & Roberts, this glitzy
confection of grey
reflective glass and
stainless steel rested on a
steel raft constructed over
all the Central side
platforms, extending
south-west to Eccleston
Bridge. Its entrance
forecourt, behind five
graceful masonry arches,
took up the site of the
parcels depot and van
loading bay next to the
former cab exit arch
and also required the
closure on 27 August
1981 of the news cinema
and its subsequent
demolition. Otherwise
the ornamented

boundary wall along
Buckingham Palace Road
was retained and
refurbished. Most of the
offices were leased in
1987 to house the
Department of Trade and
Industry.

At its south east side,
the raft accommodated
check-in facilities and a
lounge for the Gatwick
rail-air traffic. Linked to
the dedicated platforms
by escalators and a lift
and also to the main
concourse by two
escalators, this opened
on 12 January 1988. Two
additional platforms, 16
and 17, were inserted on
the site of the former
Central side cab road,
making it possible to
dedicate 13 and 14 to the
airport service. From 14
May 1984 non-stop
Gatwick trains had oper-
ated every 15 minutes.

Taxis, cars and coaches

reached the 1988 rail/air
terminal at raft level by
an access road from
Eccleston Bridge and
additional parking space
was made by extending
the raft as far as the
centre of the outer ends
of the listed LC&DR train
shed, blocking the view of
the graceful double arch.

'Victoria Place', a
72,000 sq ft shopping
mall developed by the
Heron Property Group
beneath Victoria Plaza
opened in September
1987. It was escalator
linked to the enlarged
concourse and also to the
rail/air terminal.

Above the 18 shops,
escalators and stairs led
up to a mezzanine level
'food court'. According to
its promoters, this
development was 'a
meeting place, a shopping
place, an eating place, a
pop-in place ...'

Further office space was erected above the lengthy Central Side platforms 9–19 between Eccleston Bridge and Elizabeth Bridge following a joint development agreement between the BRPB, Greycoat Group and Sir Robert McAlpine & Sons (also the main builders of Victoria Plaza). Providing 300,000 sq ft of offices and shops, this was completed early in 1992. In a nod to the railway connection, its internal road was named Bulleid Way after the SR Chief Mechanical Engineer but, in another touch of irony, it harboured commuter coaches competing with the railway.

The listed twin-arch train shed of the former LC&DR terminus was reprieved (*49, 50*) but below it the barrier line of platforms 3–6 was set back and rebuilt in zigzag form with retail units in 1985–86 and again in 2001–2 when ticket gates were installed.

After removal of parts of the dividing wall, further unity was given by construction of 'Victoria Island', a two-storey, 20,000 sq ft retail block placed across the boundary between the two stations. Completed in 1992–93, this provided those relaxing on the escalator-served terrace of its bar with a vista of the activity on the enlarged concourse below.

49

Although bereft of the glamour of its former international and Pullman services and VIP arrivals, Victoria at the beginning of the 21st century had achieved the highest throughput of passengers of all British stations and was the busiest and most profitable of the London termini, with around 209,000 passengers every weekday. Given continued growth of its traffic, it is possible that further major rebuilding will be necessary before much longer.

50

PADDINGTON

Paddington escaped major reconstruction in the 20th century. Its fine Grade 1 listed train shed, carefully restored and repainted in the late 1980s and early 1990s, looks as splendid as ever (50, 55). Brunel watches from platform 1 over his work and that of Wyatt, his architect, with a concerned gaze, in the form of John Doubleday's 1982 bronze statue (59). The initials of the once proud sole owner and operator are still evident (51, 52, 53), although the directors and managers no longer look out from the balcony of their boardroom (56).

Together with 18 other railway hotels, BR sold the Great Western Royal across the station front in 1983. It was still proudly exhibiting its GWR 'shirt button' logo in 2002! Another sale, in 1986, was the 40-acre GWR goods depot south of the Harrow Road between Westbourne Bridge and Bishops Bridge but after demolition it remained fallow until developed in 2001–2 with blocks of residential apartments, 'Paddington Central' with their own access to the station.

During 1984–86 the concourse area was enlarged by moving the heads of platforms 1–8 just over 40 yd west. Four retail units were placed along the new line and a large departure indicator set above. A new entrance and ticket hall for the Underground was built at the south east end of the concourse and the bridge at the north west end of the station giving access to the Hammersmith & City Line and suburban platforms 13–16 was rebuilt with a new ticket office. Some decried the way in which the new barrier line and indicator blocked the north westward vista down the 1854 train shed.

Resignalling (from a new IECC at Slough) and rearrangement of the approach tracks, completed in July 1993, paved the way for electrification into Heathrow Airport. Smart new Heathrow Express trains began running every 15 minutes on a 15 minute journey from 23 June 1998. At Paddington, platforms 6 and 7 were moved and widened and platform 8 repositioned. Numbers 3–11 and both main and relief lines in the approaches were all wired to provide flexibility of operation.

By the end of the 1990s, these trains were moving around 12,000 passengers in and out of Paddington daily, this and other traffic growth

51

justifying further improvements and updating in 1998–99. The 'Lawn' at the south east end of the concourse was rearranged to provide an area of passenger and retail facilities at platform and escalator-served mezzanine levels, shielded from station noise and diesel fumes by a glass wall. There were 27 flight check-in points and the entrance to the Underground and its ticket hall below were also enlarged and improved, the former given a lift and two escalators flanking wider stairs. As at Waterloo and Victoria, a mezzanine bar at the north east side of the concourse included a balcony from which customers could gaze down at the animated scene below. On the

52

53

opposite side, a new entrance to the hotel and a restaurant are available at mezzanine and first floor level respectively. After a £60m makeover, the hotel, with its splendidly-ornamented Praed Street frontage (54) reopened in 2002 as the Hilton Paddington.

Remembering the fuss about the indicator across the platform ends, a new one was erected parallel with the platforms but, as at Waterloo, its flat screen technology proved difficult to read in a high situation bathed in daylight.

56

A second phase of reconstruction, designed like the first by Nicholas Grimshaw and Partners, now awaits final approval. This involves the potentially controversial removal of the 1916 bay of the train shed above platforms 9–12. If agreed, it will provide an additional platform with heads of all platforms arranged in a continuous line across the station, long term car parking and improved taxi access. Financing would come from a 42-storey office block above the area.

57

DOMINE · DIRIGE · NOS   VIRTUTE · ET · INDUSTRIA

58

59

61

MARYLEBONE

With a traffic that has never required more than a few platforms, little Marylebone's frontage and concourse survived into the 21st century substantially unaltered. Several attempts to close it, diverting the residual traffic elsewhere and a crazy scheme to convert it to a bus and coach station served by a dedicated roadway along the approach tracks ran into the sand. Today, spruced up, bright and cheerful, its frontage Grade II listed, it retains several reminders of its parent company (60, 64). Tucked away at the eastern end is the home of the very successful Chiltern Railways. As well as their core task of serving London's north western suburbs and Buckinghamshire commuterland beyond, CR have since May 1993 restored long distance travel to this modest terminus, worked from 1998 with 100 mph diesel units reaching Birmingham in two hours. A walk westwards along the concourse reveals that the rest of the building is now more of a shopping mall and 'food court' (62) than a railway station. Those who recall the old Marylebone

62

63

64

111

65

66

cannot resist a wry smile when they discover the Marks & Spencer food shop in the former booking hall with shelves of wine bottles obscuring the 1899 oil-polished wainscot oak ticket office screen.

In March 1987 after sale with planning permission for reversion to its original role, the last BR staff left the 1899 Hotel Great Central. Listed Grade II in that year, its exterior was described as 'an exuberant display of late Victorian redbrick and terra cotta, mixing classical and "Jacobean" decorative details'. Much of the interior was then gouged out and rebuilt to five-star standards, providing 300 rooms with en suite bathrooms and an eight-storey central atrium. Opening as 'The Regent London' on 20 February 1993, it changed hands in 1995 and became 'The Landmark London'. The original GCR porte cochere, restored in 1993, still links its north entrance with the station frontage though very few guests now arrive by train (65). Inside the station, the approach tracks, platforms, barrier line and concourse underwent rearrangement and modernisation during 1990–91. New platforms replaced the former cab road and the western bay of the train shed was demolished, leaving platformed tracks 1–3 (east to west) in the other two and 4 along the west side (66). Resignalling saw the removal of the last semaphores at a London terminus and operation from an IECC at Marylebone began in October 1990.